PONY

PONY

A PLAY

SYLVAN OSWALD

NORTHWESTERN UNIVERSITY PRESS
EVANSTON, ILLINOIS

Northwestern University Press
www.nupress.northwestern.edu

Printed in the United States of America

10 9 8 7 6 5 4 3 2 1

An earlier version of "The Other Side of the Forest: *Pony*, Transmasculinity, and Generational Shift" appeared in *American Theatre* magazine as "Exuberant and Wild: The Long, Evolving Ride of Sylvan Oswald's 'Pony.'"

ISBN 978-0-8101-4865-9 (paper)
ISBN 978-0-8101-4866-6 (ebook)

Cataloging-in-Publication Data are available from the Library of Congress.

To our queer and trans elders

CONTENTS

SOFT BUTCH LANDING, A PREFACE

passing as male, a heartthrob
stone butch
trans man or male
gender nonconforming/transmasculine heartthrob
stone butch, dignified, social worker
trans man, hipster, early twenties
self-styled masculine-leaning genders
This play is a fable and its world a queer microcosm.

The first time trans identity was a conscious starting place in my work was while developing the script for *Pony* from 2005 to 2011. The list above describes the characters of *Pony* as I envisioned them, drawing on a range of identities on the spectrum between nonbinary and transmasculine. In case anyone was wondering, Pony must be irresistible.

Before that I didn't even know I was searching. My leading characters were

(a pants role)
a boy to be played by a girl
a boy
a butch woman with James Dean looks
a civic leader in a tuxedo shirt and pants.[1]

I was looking for language. I needed words to describe myself. And I needed language to describe my characters' gender identities. These lists of names and descriptors represent a history of my butch and transmasculine characters from 2000 to 2011. They are also a history of my dawning self-knowledge as a trans person, a timeline of zines I read in search of people like me, a footnote to the queer films of the 1990s to which my mother, an investigative journalist with a trauma-informed passion for truth-telling, took me to as a teenager, and an accidental group portrait of the peers who supported my attempts to put transmasculinity on stage.[2]

Touch Down

After the title, byline, and contact info on a play's cover page, you land on the landing page. You touch down, make contact with new atmosphere. The landing page defines the world you're about to enter, its who, where, and when. In the history of landing pages, things were pretty steady for a while until Caryl Churchill used a slash to mark where one character interrupts another. Was that sometime in the late '70s? Then Suzan-Lori Parks in the late '80s intervened with spells, a technique, loosely related to a rest in music, in which nonverbal energy flows between characters, indicated by the appearance of a name without any lines of dialogue, or two names stacked in alternation. Playwrights started treating the page like a score; landing pages now told you musically, *how*; readers had to learn new grammar.

My graduate playwriting program encouraged wild experimentation with all aspects of script design, and my interventions with gender were part of that conversation. We were also learning the business of playwriting, which largely conflicted with that experimentation. Trojan horse-ing one's innovation into one's script was a frequent topic.[3] Legibility was still important so as not to baffle and thereby thwart one's early readers (usually a volunteer or underpaid literary assistant). As soon as I started bringing in pages to workshop, discussions of the legibility of my characters' genders began. What was a "pants role" and why was that important? (It's a term from opera in which a female character puts on male drag to accomplish a goal, often a seduction, for a male employer. Once the effort is complete, the character reveals their drag and is "restored" to their initial gender presentation.) Would writing "butch" in 2003 be confusing to theater people? Or would it "overly limit" who could be cast in the role, thereby limiting who would produce the play? What if a producer didn't know anyone—couldn't they just cast an excellent actress? Would she have to cut her hair short, or could she just wear a ponytail? What if there was a butch person but they weren't good enough or as good as a non-butch person? I had no answers.

I probably needn't have worried since my plays were not aligned with what was then considered producible. But I didn't know whether that was my storytelling ability or my queer characters (or both). Plus, even queer theaters largely produced plays by white cis men.

If I couldn't articulate it, how could I argue for it? This was how I ended up with casting notes like "at this play's premiere, all parts were played by women," or "all parts may be played by women." Members of my writing workshop suggested that by sharing the choices from original productions, producers would get the point. In the early aughts, if I didn't explicitly state my intentions, if identity wasn't explicit on the page, the heteronormative (even homonormative) assumptions were immediate.

Even if producers did get the point, I would later learn, we might end up choosing between talented cis-het women who had no chemistry versus transmasc but untrained performers (acting schools had nothing to train them *for* since the roles did not exist as far as those educators were concerned). While I would be able to consistently cast appropriate genders for Pony and Cav (early transition and stone butch respectively, more on this below), on a couple of occasions I cast cis gay men to play the young trans man, Heath. I was wary of being considered too difficult by casting departments by insisting that they search harder. It still seemed understandable to cast a cis person before the wealth of Gen Z talent had come of age. But it didn't feel right at the time, and I can't imagine doing that now.

Butch Mentorship

Writers advocate for their people's humanity. To write a character is to summon an energy; it is to usher being-ness into the world. We do this by drawing on people we've seen and upon ourselves. My dawning concept of my gender when I started all this, tentatively and then almost proudly, was butch. I came up under the wings of my butch camp counselors (closeted for the kids), who inspired me to take up the guitar and gave me my first tube socks, and of queer-theater heroes Peggy Shaw and Lois Weaver of Split Britches, whose 1996 anthology *Split Britches: Lesbian Practice / Feminist Performance* (edited by Sue-Ellen Case) depicted a butch-femme embrace so steamy I didn't carry it around in public. Weaver was the genius femme performing, producing, directing, writing grants. Shaw, raised by drag queens and descended from legends like Gladys Bentley and Stormé DeLarverie, wrote and performed. Shaw served a kind of butch hotness to which I could aspire. I set my course and started writing roles that the two of them could play.

But who would those actors be? I certainly didn't know them. I knew one good female actor with short hair and that was it. It was one thing to have heroes, but it was another thing to find people who would work with me.

I somehow missed the entirety of the drag king moment, where I might have found willing conspirators. Drag king troupes were part of the nightlife world and performed at clubs and parties. I had a track record of pouring energy into theater instead of queer community, which was probably part of my problem.

Some Kind of Family

By 2005 I was trying to write a new play about some butches in the woods. It had roles for Peggy Shaw; for Dominique Dibbell from the Five Lesbian Brothers, who had just blown my mind in *Oedipus at Palm Springs*; and for Becca Blackwell, who I had encountered while they were doing stunts for NYC's queer radical Circus Amok (helmed by bearded woman Jennifer Miller).

I was twenty-five and had just met someone who I knew was trans for the first time. He was assigned female at birth and used male pronouns. I was nervous around him. I didn't know you could do that in life, but there he was, existing in a space between received language and his ideas of himself. I was not yet trans-identified, but this was the bewilderment I needed to begin researching transition in earnest. Shortly after, I saw Jess Barbagallo perform in Big Dance Theater's *The Other Here* and I knew I had found the youngest member of this butch—and maybe transmasculine—family. From that point forward, trans identity was the starting place for the first time in my work.

Using Fear

I used to have a lot of fear about what transition would mean for me—I bought into stereotypes about "'roid rage," aggression, and irrepressible libido (all easily managed by an adult with boundaries). I feared I would lose my relationship. In earlier drafts of *Pony* this fear and the fear of violence motivated Pony's move to a small upstate town. After a consultation with writer Jacob Anderson-Minshall set up by Oregon's Portland Center Stage around a 2008 workshop, I understood that the notion that a trans person would leave their community to transition was antiquated. Nor was it a trope the community wished to reinscribe—the message should be one of inclusion. I revised Pony's backstory so that the town was his first stop after serving time. Leaving prison would require life changes, and the prison industrial complex paralleled *Woyzeck*'s world, in which the title character is acted upon by agents of local military and medical establishments. I had repurposed the skeleton of Georg Büchner's unfinished 1837 play during a desperate moment in 2005 when I needed more propulsion for *Pony*'s action. The shape of *Pony*, the fear that Pony shows up with, arcing toward the release of that fear, is indebted to the writer-directors who adapted Vito Russo's 1981 book *The Celluloid Closet* into the 1995 documentary of the same name. After viewing the film, which depicts the history of queer and trans death onscreen, I knew I had to confront that grand narrative.

Tipping

It wasn't until I piloted a course in trans theater in spring 2022 that I engaged with the idea of the "transgender tipping point." That was the headline when Laverne Cox owned the cover of *Newsweek* (June 9, 2014). The issue dropped about four years after I came out and publicly changed my name in time for the world premiere of *Pony* in Chicago at About Face, directed and creatively produced by Bonnie Metzgar.

Since that 2011 premiere, I had been trying not to think too much about why *Pony,* a classroom staple for many of my colleagues, had only received one production while plays of similar vintage by my peers had been produced repeatedly. No, it wasn't exactly an easy play. There was the heightened language, maybe the *Woyzeck* element was a little too much for some people, and it was highly likely that companies didn't have butch or trans actors in their communities—or didn't know or find out if they did. Maybe they didn't know who in their audience would show up for a story about transmasculine characters. It didn't help that mixed reviews from the Chicago press had little context for trans content. There were no pull quotes.

In the intervening years, I was happy to witness other trans writers having plays produced in highly visible venues such as the Actors Theatre of Louisville, and through small-but-mighty New York companies such as the National Asian-American Theatre Company, Rattlestick Theater, and Colt Coeur.[4] I also made a few changes to the script here and there to reflect my deepening knowledge of trans experience. In early spring of 2022 I was approached by actor-producer Dave Register, who was seeking to produce *Pony* in a new theater festival he was starting in Portland, Maine. He had been privately coaching a transmasc local actor and had begun to use *Pony* for scene work as suggested by Jess Barbagallo, a former castmate. His affection for the play had inspired him to program it alongside Annie Baker's *Body Awareness* and Antoinette Nwandu's *Pass Over* for the inaugural Portland Theater Festival. Later that summer the Cutting Ball Theater in San Francisco reached out hoping to program *Pony* for an opening in their season. These were startling and welcome developments.

Back in that pilot class, we—a group of cis, nonbinary, and trans UCLA graduate theater students and I—were attempting to construct a timeline of trans theater that I could use in a future class for undergrads. We included elders like Warhol alum Jackie Curtis and Bay Area stalwart Red Jordan Arobateau. The timeline exercise yielded an undeniable explanation: *Pony* premiered before the tipping point. It was a relief, the way a diagnosis can be, despite its still disappointing reality.

And the feeling that followed was grief. As someone born at the cusp of the Gen X and Millennial generations, I had often thought of myself as a beneficiary of the queers who came before, be they those who quietly survived, those who didn't, or those who acted up in protest. It hadn't occurred to me, despite having taught for so many years at that point, that I probably had some of that wall-breaking dust on me too. Looking around that room of trans, nonbinary, queer, and yes, even cis-het students who had just mapped out a history of trans theater, it was undeniable that the tipping point was a threshold worthy of celebration.

This is some of what *Pony* is about—how we relate to our own and each other's struggles to exist as ourselves across time. At a moment when trans rights are under siege in the United States, we need the wisdom of everyone we've got.

Los Angeles, 2023

NOTES

1. The first cascade lists descriptions of the transmasc characters Pony, Cav, and Heath from *Pony* manuscripts from 2006–9, 2010–11, and 2019–22. The second cascade refers to characters in my earlier plays *Goat* Songs, 2000 (characters #1 and #2 refer to Fergus); *Desmond or Abraham and Frances*, 2001 (#3 is Desmond; the script also contains the note "At this play's premiere, all of the parts were played by women"); *Plutonics*, 2002 (#4, Constance); and *Two Spent Swimmers*, 2003 (#5, Rom).
2. My zine reading evolved with my gender, from *Sassy* to *Girls Like Us* to *Original Plumbing*. My mom took me to see *Go Fish* (dir. Rose Troche, 1994), *The Celluloid*

Closet (dir. Rob Epstein and Jeffrey Friedman, 1995, based on Vito Russo's 1981 book), *The Incredibly True Adventure of Two Girls in Love* (dir. Maria Maggenti, 1995), and *The Watermelon Woman* (dir. Cheryl Dunye, 1996). In 1997 Ellen DeGeneres came out on her TV show a few months before I graduated high school. *Boys Don't Cry* (dir. Kimberly Peirce) came out in 1999; *By Hook or by Crook* (dir. Harry Dodge and Silas Howard) came out in 2001.

3. I detail this influence and a personal history of plays on the page in the essay "Cut Piece," created for 3 Hole Press (Rachel Kauder Nalebuff's genre-agnostic play publishing project, now concluded). Should their site close at some point, I will post the essay at my personal website until it can appear elsewhere. https://www.3holepress.org/cutpiece.
4. An account of the movement toward greater trans visibility in US theater appears in my essay "Towards a Trans Theater," included in *The Methuen Drama Handbook of Gender and Theatre*, edited by Sean Metzger and Roberta Mock.

PRODUCTION HISTORY

Pony was developed with support from Millay Arts, a Thurber House fellowship from the Ohio State University, a Jerome Fellowship from the Playwrights' Center in Minneapolis, and the McCarter Theatre's retreat.

The roles of Cav, Pony, and Heath were inspired by performers Peggy Shaw, Becca Blackwell, and Jess Barbagallo, respectively.

Readings were sponsored by Karina Mangu-Ward, New York Theatre Workshop, and About Face Theatre. Oregon's Portland Center Stage produced a workshop at JAW/West, where it was directed by Ken Rus Schmoll.

Chicago's About Face Theatre produced the world premiere of *Pony* at Chopin Theatre in April 2011. It was directed by Bonnie Metzgar, with dramaturgy by Eric Hoff; set design by Tom Burch; lighting design by Lee Fiskness; sound design by Misha Fiskel; props by Maria Defabo; fight choreography by Derek Gasper; and costume design by David Hyman. Kimberly Miller was the stage manager. The cast was as follows:

Marie .... Kristina Valada-Viars
Pony .... Kelli Simpkins
Stell .... Jessica Hudson
Heath .... Matthew Sherbach
Cav .... Janet Ulrich-Brooks

PLAYWRIGHT'S NOTE, 2025

Pony was written, revised, and premiered over the years 2005–2011, and reflected my understanding of intra-LGBTQ+ politics during that time. Because community awareness (and the world's) has evolved since the 2011 draft, I have made a few updates to these dynamics.

PONY

CHARACTERS

Marie (she/her), intellectual femme, a waitress, thirties
Pony (he/him), nonbinary/transmasculine heartthrob, mid- to late thirties
Stell (she/her), a sales agent, thirties
Heath (he/him), trans man, early twenties
Cav (she/her), stone butch, dignified, social worker, late fifties

SETTING

On the other side of the forest from *Woyzeck*

TIME

Now and *Woyzeck*

NOTES

A double dash with a period (--.) indicates a wordless beat.
If needed, an intermission could be added after scene 19.

SOURCE

This is a response to the 1837 play *Woyzeck*, by Georg Büchner, who died before completing it. Of the heap of manuscript pages assembled by different editors, one critic writes, "Strictly speaking, [this play] does not exist."

[A dense wood outside a fictional county seat, possibly in upstate New York, 250 miles north of the affluent South City. Industry has left behind some vaguely military buildings, yet new life is slowly returning. A few buses serve the town. The bus station sits near a newsstand and a social services field office. Ramshackle houses and a rusty fairground are tucked away in the woods. There is a river. And a backroads bar.

The set is a landscape of wide, old, rough boards isolated in the darkness. All the settings in the play should be conjured from these boards. The clothes people wear look like what you'd expect in a depressed rural town, but there's something, maybe in the tailoring at the shoulders or maybe the silhouette, that suggests a hint of another time, of history hovering beneath the surface.]

PROLOGUE: SUNRISE

[A man emerges from the woods through early morning fog. This is PONY. *He pulls a beat-up tin from his pocket. Holds it a moment. Puts it away and walks on.]*

1. RIVER BANK

[MARIE, *measuring the distance across the river. Wading in. Seeing what it would be like to throw a knife. It's a creative act—imagining what might have happened here. After a little while,* PONY *enters and watches.* MARIE *resists breaking her concentration. Then, finally:*]

MARIE: Seems pretty, right?

PONY: Sure.

MARIE: You'd never know—

PONY: What.

MARIE: Something terrible happened here.

PONY: --. What are you doing.

MARIE: --. Trying to figure it out.

PONY: Or trying to get pneumonia.

MARIE: --. Can't get it from water.

PONY: --. You could drown.

MARIE: I can swim.

PONY: Hm. Isn't this for the sheriff?

MARIE: They don't know the half of it.

PONY: They catch the guy?

MARIE: Yeah, but that don't make me feel any better.

PONY: What else is there to know?

MARIE: --.

PONY: --.

MARIE: Everything.

PONY: --.

MARIE: --.

PONY: Something's gonna kill me I don't know what.

MARIE: No different from anyone else.

PONY: Don't you get flashes of your death?
Mine's not natural.

MARIE: You don't know.

PONY: That drop in your gut. The bottom falling out. I wake up with that feeling.

MARIE: Have we met?

PONY: Oh—

MARIE: It's okay—

PONY: I shouldn't have—

[They hold eye contact a moment. He breaks it. And goes.]

MARIE: Wait—

[His words echo in her head—strange. She comes to the edge of the water, grabs her towel, and rubs herself dry, as much as that's possible in jeans. She pauses a moment. Thinks she sees something in the distance.]

2. NEWSSTAND

[STELL *minds her newsstand near the bus stop. A tinny radio plays. It's the all-purpose general store for this neck of the woods. The newsstand scenes all have a slightly Chaplinesque rhythm and physicality.*

STELL *checks the time. Sound of a bus arriving. She looks hopeful: customers.*

HEATH *enters. He is a young man, casually but expensively dressed. He carries a plastic woven shopping bag. That's his hipster suitcase.*]

STELL: Where you coming from?

[*No response.*]

STELL: Hello. And welcome.
Might I interest you in a—

HEATH: No. Thank you.

[STELL *is miffed. She checks the time again, and seeing no other customers, shutters the stand.*

HEATH *realizes he's in the middle of nowhere.*]

HEATH: Oh hey, do you happen to know—

[*Too late.* STELL *hangs a LUNCH sign and heads out.*

Damn. HEATH *checks his watch, and sits to wait for her return.*]

3. ROADHOUSE

[*Cyndi Lauper's "Money Changes Everything" comes on loud.* MARIE *sings along softly to the first verse of the song while inspecting her face in a compact mirror.* PONY, *out of her view, sits with a beer and pretends not to listen.* STELL *arrives at* MARIE*'s seat with drinks for the two of them.* MARIE *notices* PONY.]

STELL: I told them to turn it down.
Hey, were you singing?

MARIE: Me?

STELL: Thought I heard your voice.

MARIE: Funny.

STELL: What's up.

MARIE: I saw smoke outside on my way here.

STELL: Again?

MARIE: Wonder where it's coming from.

STELL: It's not coming from anywhere.
What's going on with you?

MARIE: Lots of things.
Did you see a new guy over there?

STELL: Where.

MARIE: Thought I saw a guy I didn't recognize.

STELL: And smoke outside and you're singing along in the bar?

MARIE: So? Here's money.

STELL: Oh I got this round.

MARIE: Stell, you don't got it.

STELL: I do. I got it.

MARIE: Fine. Thank you.

STELL: Are you going to tell me how things are going?

MARIE: I did.

STELL: With your boyfriend?

MARIE: He fucks me too hard.

STELL: Too hard.

MARIE: Look—you wanna pry? That's what's going on. It's distracting.

STELL: What are you going to do about it?

MARIE: I don't know.

STELL: How about—tell him?

MARIE: I can't.

STELL: How about—ask for it soft?

MARIE: Yeah—

STELL: Can't say no?

MARIE: Could you keep it down?

STELL: Oh that guy's not listening.

PONY: Oh I'm totally listening.

STELL: Asshole!

MARIE: Don't listen, okay?

PONY: Well don't talk about sex so loud.

STELL: What a jerk.

PONY: I'll just mind my own business.

MARIE: Good idea.

PONY: If you want any advice—

STELL: From you?

PONY: —from my deep well of experience—

STELL [*to* MARIE]: Cocky!

MARIE: Yeah but a little cute.

STELL: Naw—

MARIE: Yeah. A little. So—my cunt hurts.

STELL: From when he fucks you too hard?

MARIE: Yeah.

STELL: I wish I could help. I really do. It's too bad.

[MARIE *drains her drink.*]

MARIE: You wanna help?

STELL [*blushing*]: Yeah.

MARIE: Get me another one.

STELL [*disappointed*]: Already? Okay.

[STELL *goes to the bar.* MARIE *looks over at* PONY, *who feigns not looking at her.* MARIE *approaches.*]

MARIE: So who are you.

PONY: Pony. I'm new up here.

MARIE: Well that's nice. From where. Oh let me guess—South City.

PONY: Oh hell no. Maybe twenty years ago—

MARIE: Thought you might be the type.

PONY: When I lived there I was way out in the boroughs.

MARIE: Oh. You must like the fresh air.

PONY: I like the quiet.

MARIE: There's starting to be artists here now. Wait, was that a hint?

PONY: No. What's that saying—first the artists and the queers?

MARIE: I don't know.

PONY: When areas start gentrifying?

MARIE: That's probably not happening here.

PONY: I wonder.

[STELL *swoops in with* MARIE*'s drink.*]

STELL: Cheers.

MARIE: Thanks.

PONY: Little early for the second whiskey.

[*A hot look between* MARIE *and* PONY. STELL *sees this.*]

MARIE: Nobody asked.

[*And another. This is unacceptable to* STELL.]

STELL: Excuse me, Marie, I gotta go back to work. Don't you?

MARIE: Worked breakfast.

STELL: Right.

MARIE: And I'll do it again tomorrow.

STELL: See ya later?

MARIE: Prob'ly.

STELL: Okay.
Be good.

MARIE [*not turning*]: Bye.

[STELL *exits.*]

PONY: So. Marie.

MARIE: Yeah so you know my name whatever.

PONY: What were you doing at the river—

MARIE: Already told you.

PONY: —walking into the water like that?

MARIE: Did I scare you?

PONY: You said there was something the sheriff didn't know.

MARIE: New guy's got a lot of questions.

PONY: A fella's got to know the lay of the land.

MARIE: I see.

PONY: And I'm fascinated.
You're like a detective.

[MARIE *conceals a blush.*]

PONY: So what's the big mystery?

MARIE [*rhetorical*]: If you commit a crime of passion, can you be innocent?

PONY: I guess it depends.

MARIE: I say, you can.

PONY: But you're still "committing" the crime.

MARIE: Don't forget insanity.

PONY: Right. Insanity.

MARIE: Our killer. The one I'm following. Killed his girlfriend. Rivers of blood from a single slash. Police said it was well done. He knew just where to put the knife.

PONY: How would he know that?

MARIE: You study up.

PONY: Passion's no excuse then.

MARIE: Especially if she didn't actually cheat like he thought.

PONY: How do you know?

MARIE: I just know. And I've done extensive interviews with people from town.

PONY: So now you go down to the river—

MARIE: To reconstruct. He's disaffected, alienated, stone-cold broke, and working a number of menial jobs. And then he starts thinking his woman's running around. What happens in that moment—that snap—that blink. How do you get to that point?

PONY: Do things like that happen around here—often?

MARIE: Well, we're scraping by.

PONY: Is this—what you do?

MARIE: "Do"? Like do for a living?

PONY: You wait tables, but what do you "do"?

MARIE: This 'n' that. And this.

[PONY *looks a little dubious.*]

MARIE: Still fascinated?

PONY: I—

MARIE: Because I still don't know anything about you.

PONY: I don't really like to talk about myself.

MARIE: I can tell. Why this town, then.

PONY: Thought I could find some peace.
Just be myself. Be my real self.

MARIE: What makes you think it'll be better here?

PONY: I'm just hoping. Could be my last chance.

[*Beat.* PONY *gets up.*]

I gotta go.

MARIE: I'll find you.

PONY: Don't. You're taken.

MARIE: I do what I want. I'll find you.

PONY: Apparently it's a small town.

[*Strains of the next jukebox song—something like Fleetwood Mac's "Dreams," when the top of the first chorus wells up.*]

4. SOCIAL SERVICES OFFICE

[CAV *is* PONY*'s social worker.*]

PONY: So, what's the deal with that experiment you told me about.

CAV: It's a study. You still interested?

PONY: Maybe. I get paid?

CAV: Fifteen dollars an hour.

PONY: That'll work.

CAV: It's like a job. You have to come in or sometimes we come to you to see how you're doing, a couple times a week, while you keep looking for a job.

PONY: And can you get fired?

CAV: Only if you miss your appointments.

PONY: So what's it about?

CAV: People getting back on their feet after time inside.
People starting over. Like you.

PONY: Like me.

CAV: --.

PONY: How many people you got?

CAV: I can't tell you that.

PONY: A lot? A hundred?

CAV: More.

PONY: Wow.

CAV: Yes. Well I have a staff.

PONY: Really? This place is, like, dead.

CAV: Funding is—well—you know. So they work from the institute in town. I come out here once a week.

PONY: In the study, are you gonna use our names and tell about our backgrounds?

CAV: I can change the name if you prefer. It'll just be published among scholars—people you'd never run into.

PONY: But why are you doing this?

CAV: I guess the study asks, Can people change? What does it mean to change?

PONY: What do you think?

CAV: I don't know.
Right now you're doing good. You're putting out applications, right?

PONY: Yeah! Sure.

CAV: What have you done.

PONY: Do you need to give me the third degree?

CAV: This is how it works.

PONY: Okay. Well. I went to town and I checked out the hardware store. And the diner. And the feed store.

CAV: Checked out?

PONY: I went in. And asked if they were hiring.

CAV: And?

PONY: No! They weren't.

CAV: Sounds like that's making you angry.

PONY: Of course!

CAV: All they did was say that they weren't hiring. It had nothing to do with you.

PONY: Oh yeah? I don't know. It was like [*a look up and down*] "Not at the moment."

CAV: That's just small-town bullshit, don't you think?

PONY: Fucking discrimination is what it is.

CAV: Against the unemployed?

PONY: You know what I'm fucking talking about.

CAV: You think they can tell there's something different about you?

PONY: Maybe.

CAV: I can't tell.

PONY: Well look at you.

CAV: What about me.

PONY: Look at us.

CAV: Two good-lookin' dudes—

[PONY *lets that hang, a little awkward/irritated, but decides to move on.*]

PONY: When I was getting out and I heard of you, I didn't think it would be in this kind of place. All these military, all these medical complexes in the area.

CAV: What did you imagine.

PONY: Some hippy-dippy fruit stand run by some Statue of Liberty who'd want to date me.

CAV: You couldn't've gone to your sister, huh?

PONY: She doesn't get it.

CAV: Sorry to hear that.

PONY: Yeah. Hey, what are your pronouns?

CAV: She and her.

PONY: Okay.

CAV: It's one thing I never pushed.

PONY: Why not?

CAV: I don't—
It was—
another time.

PONY: Was that too personal?

CAV: We can talk about it—another time.

[*Beat.* CAV *looks out a window.*]

PONY: Why do you have those stones on your desk?

CAV: These? I pick them up when I go to the beach. Don't know why. I like looking at them.

PONY: Me too.

5. NEWSSTAND

[STELL *is rushing back from lunch. She almost trips over* HEATH, *who has spread out, kind of resting his eyes. As soon as he sees her, he springs into action.*]

HEATH: Hi!

STELL: Good day.

HEATH: Did you have a nice lunch?

STELL: It was satisfactory.

[*She gets situated back at her stand, taking down the sign and resuming her reading.*]

HEATH: What are you reading there?

STELL: Some dark shit.

HEATH: But is it porn?

STELL: I'd say so.

HEATH: Cool.

STELL: Can I help you?

HEATH: Can I buy a water?

STELL: One dollar.

HEATH: Thank you sooo much.

STELL: You weren't planning on sleeping here, like tonight, were you.

HEATH: I was waiting for you to come back from lunch. What makes you think I'm staying in this shithole tonight?

STELL: By shithole are you referring to the entire town or this particular area?

HEATH: I thought this was a public park.

STELL: You shouldn't close your eyes around here. It's not safe.

HEATH: Oh I'll be fine.

STELL: What are you doing here?

HEATH: Oh that's right, this is like a small town and everybody knows everything about everybody so, like, who's the stranger.

STELL: --.

HEATH: I'm here to find someone.

STELL: Who.

HEATH: Kind of a father figure. Who didn't raise me. But who I just hope is gonna wanna know me. I don't need taking care of. But I can't live at home anymore and—

STELL: Who is it.

HEATH: Wait wait I don't want to make it this shocking surprise, I mean, it's surprising that I'm showing up but I want to do this in my own way.

STELL: Well—whoever it is—I'm sure I can help.

HEATH: Really?!

STELL: I'm very helpful.

HEATH [*laughs*]: Are you, like, the person who knows everybody's business?

STELL [*laughing with him*]: That's my business!

[STELL *continues to laugh for a second and then totally stops.*]

HEATH: [*Laughs a second too long, then notices* STELL*'s not laughing.*]

STELL: It'll be a thousand dollars.

HEATH: No way.

STELL: --.

HEATH: Five hundred.

STELL: Don't insult me. Eight hundred and you pay half up front.

HEATH: Six hundred, half up front.

STELL: Seven, half up front.

HEATH: Fine.

STELL: There's an ATM—

HEATH: I fucking got it, okay? Jesus.

[HEATH *pulls out a wad of cash.*]

STELL: Look at you.

HEATH: How are we gonna do this?

STELL: You pay me.

HEATH: And.

STELL: And I find Daddy.

HEATH: It's not Daddy like that.

STELL: Does Daddy have a name?

HEATH: It's different now. Changed.

STELL: Daddy with a name change.

HEATH: And maybe some—other changes.

STELL: Uh huh. Well, we got options.

HEATH: More than one?

STELL: Two.

HEATH: Good.

STELL: One at a time.

[STELL *puts her hand out for the money.* HEATH *hands it over.*]

6. CARNIVAL

[*Evening.* PONY *and* MARIE *have gone to a carnival on a date.*]

[MARIE, *alone for a moment, surveys the carnival scene. As with most things, it becomes part of her investigation. After a few beats, sounds of the carnival, and* PONY *comes back her way.*]

PONY: I'm gonna win you a stuffed snake!

MARIE: Now what am I gonna do with that?

PONY: Oh—wait! House of Mirrors! I'm gonna go in there.

MARIE: You'll fuck yourself up. Never get out.

PONY: Oh, you don't wanna get fucked up?

MARIE: Not like that!

PONY: A hundred of me staring back.

MARIE: That's scary!

PONY: You're right it's totally scary.

[*Sound of a rollercoaster.*]

PONY: Where's your boyfriend tonight?

MARIE: Working.

PONY: Late?

MARIE: Night shift.

[*Sound of winning: ding ding ding ding.*]

PONY: Why didn't you want me to know your name in the bar?

MARIE: You were a stranger!

PONY: That's a lame excuse.

MARIE: I think my name is boring. And now it's the same name as the dead girl. Across town.

PONY: You have the same name? No wonder you're obsessed.

MARIE: Hey—

PONY: I mean, why don't you change it?

MARIE: My name?

PONY: If you don't like it.

MARIE: I can't.

PONY: It's easy. Pull it from the air. Tell me a new one.

MARIE: I can't.

PONY: --. I changed my name.

MARIE: From what.

PONY: Can't tell you.

MARIE: Oh, now you're so tough.

PONY: Yeah I am.

[*Sound of fireworks.*]

MARIE: Why'd you change it?

PONY: Rite of passage.

MARIE: From boy to man?

PONY: You could say.

MARIE: Rather than brand some hussy's name on your ass, change your own name, huh?

PONY: Kind of.

MARIE: I like that. Clever. So what was it before.

PONY [*5 percent defensive*]: I said, don't ask.

MARIE: What if I wanna kiss you.

PONY: You're drunk.

MARIE: Come here.

[PONY *goes to her. A kiss.*]

PONY: We shouldn't be doing this, should we?

MARIE: I'm taken.

PONY: So I've heard.
Here.

MARIE: What's this.

PONY: Stones I found.

MARIE: Oooh.

7. NEWSSTAND

[*A little later.* HEATH *has some magic. And he's worked it. Now he and* STELL *are looking at the porn together.*]

HEATH: I'm impressed.

STELL: You need a real professional photographer—

HEATH: to fit so many dicks—

STELL: thank you—

HEATH: and still retain the detail.

[CAV *walks by on her way home from work.*]

STELL: The heat—

CAV [*to* STELL]: Hey.

STELL: Hey. [*When* CAV *is past*] Daddy #1.

HEATH: What?

STELL: Go—now's your chance!

HEATH: You didn't finish telling me! Which one is this?

STELL: Cav.

HEATH [*testing out the name in the air*]: Cav—

STELL: What—that's wrong?

HEATH: I—don't know.

STELL: Look kid, I'm late—hurry up!

[HEATH *runs after* CAV. *A pause.* CAV *comes back onstage.* HEATH *is scrambling behind. Surprised/confused eye contact between* HEATH *and* STELL.]

CAV: Stell. Have there been any letters for me.

[STELL*'s stand is also a default post office.*]

STELL: Not today, friend.

CAV: Really. Okay. Thanks.
How's it going, honey?

STELL: Don't call me that.

CAV: Are you okay?

STELL: I'm great. Thank you.

CAV: When can we—

STELL: I'll call you. [*Louder*] Where you headed?

CAV: Bus north. One last client. See ya tomorrow.

[STELL *winks at* CAV. CAV *exits.*]

STELL: Well? That bus is leaving!

HEATH: I'm trying not to be too impulsive!

STELL: Too late! [*Starts closing the stand*] Shit shit shit. I really gotta go.

[STELL *begins to leave.*]

HEATH: Can we have a meeting about this tomorrow?

STELL [*from almost offstage*]: Don't sleep outside, ya dumbass!

[HEATH *pauses a moment, then runs off after* CAV.]

8. CARNIVAL, CONT'D

[PONY *and* MARIE *are still on their date at the carnival.*]

MARIE: When I think about what he did to her I get all hot.

PONY: That guy who killed his girlfriend?

MARIE: Yeah.

PONY: Do you ever have normal fantasies?

MARIE: This one is better.

PONY: But it's violent.

MARIE: And yet you love the House of Mirrors.

PONY: I mean—

MARIE: Don't you want to know what I think about?

PONY: Yeah, but—

MARIE: He had to think about the perfect weapon.

PONY: I bet he wasn't thinking all that much—

MARIE: Could he stand to put his hands around her throat?
Could he pull a trigger?
Could he—

PONY: You like to think about doing it—being him.

MARIE: I—

PONY: Or do you like to think about being her—

[MARIE *takes a step back, considers.*]

MARIE: A little of both, I guess.

PONY: --.

MARIE: What about you?

PONY: What?

MARIE: Which one?

PONY: Neither!

MARIE: --.

PONY: I'm not—like that—I would never—

MARIE: You would never—

PONY: --.

9. BUS

[CAV *looks out the window of a bus. Sound of the bus door closing.* CAV *relaxes. Sound of knocking, the door opening. And closing.* HEATH *is there. The bus lurches forward. Going north.* CAV *sees* HEATH *and tenses up again.*]

HEATH: Mind if I sit here?

CAV: Sure.

HEATH: Thanks.

[*They sit in silence.*]

HEATH: God, don't they clean these things?

[CAV *doesn't respond, hopes* HEATH *gets the hint.*]

HEATH: I'm Heath.

CAV: Hi.

[CAV *looks out the window.*]

HEATH: Nice to meet you.

[*Will* CAV *reciprocate?*]

Where's home for you?

CAV: Town.

HEATH: I'm from South City.

CAV [*a snort*]: What are you doing up here then?

HEATH: Visiting.

CAV: Oh.

HEATH: What are you doing?

CAV: Work.

HEATH: Do you think up north will ever be as fancy as South City?

CAV: South City was a goddamn dump once too. It all evolves.

HEATH: But why do things tend toward gentrifying? Isn't there that law of physics—entropy increases? Things rot and die?

CAV: I don't know.

HEATH: Well maybe after some time all the rich people rot and die. I mean, they die. People steal from them, their fancy things go to seed—

CAV [*attention out the window*]: Yeah.

HEATH: Sorry. You look like you could use some quiet.

CAV: Thank you. For noticing that.

HEATH: I'm super perceptive. I have to be. Because I'm. Me. So.

CAV: Perceptive. That's what I was thinking.

[CAV *turns toward the window again.* HEATH *beams.*]

10. MARIE'S BEDROOM

[MARIE *and* STELL *back to back on* MARIE*'s bed.* MARIE *holds the stones* PONY *gave her.* STELL *looks tortured.*]

MARIE: These stones don't shine.

STELL: What sort you got?

MARIE: Guess.

STELL: I can't.

MARIE: Shut your eyes tight. Yeah, keep 'em like that.

STELL: Girls like us don't get the shiny kind. We get the dumps. We get the broken bits. Let me see.

MARIE: No! Girls like us can get hot kisses. I was with him so long tonight! Starin'—

STELL: You got to watch not to let anybody know—

MARIE: Nobody is gonna know what—

STELL: —what—

MARIE: Nobody is gonna know what I want!

STELL: They are if you keep starin'.

MARIE: No one saw.

STELL: That's what you think.
Either way—that's a big mess.
Lemme see those stones.

MARIE: You know what, it's been a long day, Stell. I think I gotta go to bed.
I don't need any more company tonight.

STELL: You sure?

MARIE: Yeah.

STELL: Don't you need me to rub your arms?

MARIE: Not tonight.

STELL: Oh. Okay.

MARIE: What are you going to do?

STELL: Go home. I don't know.

MARIE: You going to be okay?

STELL: Oh stop it. I'll be fine. I just changed my sheets. It'll be nice.

MARIE: Bye then.

STELL: Bye.

[STELL *goes.* MARIE *picks up her mirror.*]

MARIE: I can still see her looking at me with knives in 'er eyes. Or is it just me reflectin'. Like I am the knife.

11. OUTSIDE THE CARNIVAL

[*Dawn.* HEATH *is curled up, sleeping on the ground, his plastic shopping bag as a pillow.* PONY *walks past him at a fast pace.* STELL *is chasing* PONY. *She catches up to him.* HEATH *curls himself up even smaller so they don't notice him, and watches.*]

STELL: Look, I know I don't know you. I don't know anything about you.

PONY: We met this morning. I'm a very nice guy.

STELL: And you're new here—

PONY: What is this. Who are you?

STELL: —so I know you don't know what you're doing.

PONY: Excuse me?

STELL: You were with Marie tonight.

PONY: At the carnival. Who cares?

STELL: She has a boyfriend.

PONY: That doesn't seem to bother her.

STELL: He's bad news.

PONY: Well so am I.

STELL: And so am I.

PONY: Sounds like we should all be good friends.

STELL: He gets crazy. She gets crazy. They both do. People can get hurt.

PONY: Why are you telling me this.

STELL: I'm just the messenger.

PONY: Yeah I bet.

[STELL *takes a strategic pause.*]

STELL: I'm cool. I look out for people. So, here's some free advice. You think there's something between you—some kind of special air. But that's her. She's got gravity that pulls people in. It's not love. It's something else. She's not yours. She doesn't belong to—no one belongs to anyone around here. You work and you fuck and you get paid maybe. But no one's hiring ex-cons, Pony. Not when there's unblemished losers to go around. You think that no one knew? This town doesn't need another guy like you. And neither does Marie.

PONY: Stell, as long as you live, I don't think you'll ever meet a guy. Like. Me. What a fucking welcome. I'm going home. To sleep. By myself. Goodbye.

[STELL *stands in his path.*]

STELL: Oh am I in your way?

[PONY *storms around her and off toward home.*
Once he's gone, STELL *exits, at a clip.*
HEATH *finally exhales, eyes wide.*]

12. SOCIAL SERVICES OFFICE

[CAV *sitting at her desk.* PONY *hurries in.*]

PONY: I know I'm a little late—

CAV: You drunk?

PONY: I'm fine.

CAV: I can smell it.

PONY: And?

CAV: Look, one of the rules of the study is sober interviews. I have to disqualify this.

PONY: That mean I don't get paid?

CAV: Right.

PONY: But I showed up!

CAV: Showing up isn't enough.

PONY: What is this, medical? Government? I had ONE beer!

CAV: One?

PONY: Yeah.

CAV: One.

PONY: Look. I need this.

CAV: Fine.

PONY: I'm not an alcoholic, I just had a beer.

CAV: Okay.

PONY: Okay?

CAV: Who did you have a beer with?

PONY: You're not my mother.

CAV: Oh! Let's talk about your mother.

PONY: Fuck you.

CAV: I'm serious. Or your sister.

PONY: Fuck them. Fuck you.

CAV: Who you have a drink with is part of who you are. You want to do this?

PONY: A woman.

CAV: Someone new?

PONY: Yeah.

CAV: Who is she?

PONY: Trouble.

CAV: How do you know?

PONY: That's what comes my way.

CAV: So if you know she's trouble, what are you going to do about it?

PONY: See her tonight.

CAV: That's soon.

PONY: She's hot.

CAV: So if Trouble is hot it doesn't matter that she's trouble?

PONY: Right.

CAV: I see.

PONY: I mean, it's nothing. We'll just mess around.

CAV: You mean have sex?

PONY: I don't know. Whatever. Have fun.
How much longer is this?

CAV: You want to get paid?

PONY: Yeah.

CAV: Forty-five minutes.

PONY: Okay.

CAV: Listen, there's something I wanted to talk to you about.

PONY: What.

CAV: Why did you take those stones off my desk?

PONY: Now you're accusing me of shit.

CAV: You were my last client of the week. I came in on Monday and they were gone.

PONY: Maybe you had a break-in. That you didn't know about.

CAV: Until now.

[PONY *is caught.*]

CAV: Those meant a lot to me.

PONY: --.

CAV: Can I have them back?

PONY: You said you just picked 'em up random.

CAV: I did.

PONY: Why didn't you say that they mattered?

CAV: That would have been personal.

PONY: And there are professional boundaries . . .

CAV: Absolutely.

PONY: I don't know where they are.

CAV: That's disappointing.

PONY: Someone took them from me.

CAV: How did that feel.

PONY: I mean, I gave them away. As a gift.

CAV: Weren't yours to give.

PONY: I know.

CAV: Okay.

PONY: You still disappointed?

CAV: I am.

PONY: I'm sorry.

CAV: That hurt my feelings.

PONY: Is this about feelings.

CAV: You know what? Yeah, it is.

PONY: You gonna fire me?

CAV: You never got what you wanted huh?

PONY: --.

CAV: Things were kept from you.

PONY: When.

CAV: Then. When you were young.

PONY: --.

--.

--.

CAV: It's okay.

PONY: Should I tell her.

CAV: Who.

PONY: Marie. Should I tell her. About me.

CAV: Tell her what.

PONY: That I'm—complicated.

CAV: She probably knows that.

PONY: Stop smiling! [*Stifles a laugh.*]

CAV: Tell her what.

PONY: Oh god.

CAV: Suppose you did. Tell her. Something personal. Vulnerable.

PONY: That I have a record.

CAV: That's one thing.

PONY: She could just be gone.

CAV: You want to hold on tight.

PONY: I think so.

CAV: Suppose you told her.

PONY: It's too soon.

CAV: So, maybe later.

PONY: Maybe not.

13. MARIE'S BEDROOM

[PONY *and* MARIE *making out on* MARIE*'s bed. She tries to unbutton his shirt. He deflects her and stays in the moment. She goes for his zipper. He deflects that gently too.*]

MARIE: Do you like this?

PONY: So much.

MARIE [*reaching for him*]: So may I—

PONY: I'm—old-fashioned.

MARIE: Does that mean I should stop?

PONY: No—

MARIE: Are you seeing other people?

PONY: No, but you are.

MARIE: Like that double standard?

PONY : It's not fair.

[*A kiss.*]

MARIE: Do you feel better now?

PONY: A little . . .

MARIE: When we first met you said death was somewhere near you.

PONY: Maybe you could forget that I said that.

MARIE: Do you still feel it?

PONY: I feel like the ice is thin.

MARIE: And you could fall through?

PONY: I'm changing the subject to . . .

MARIE: Pretend I'm not here—like confession—

PONY: I've never gone—

MARIE: Okay me neither but I think you sit side by side and there's a screen between you and the priest or whatever. And you just confess it. You just say it.

PONY: This is weird.

MARIE: We're just in my room. You and me.

PONY: It's too soon for secrets.

MARIE: Do I look like I scare easy?

[PONY *is moved by this, kisses* MARIE.]

MARIE: Here. You can pretend you're not even you. Imagine you're—
Put a box around yourself—
the idea of yourself—
and set you aside for a minute.
Then start to envision another man.
A man on the verge.
He can't keep it all inside anymore.
The frustration, the bitterness, the voices.
What does he say?

PONY: Who is this?

MARIE: Just try.

PONY: I don't hear voices.

MARIE: It's okay—this is just a way for you to maybe tell me what you're afraid to tell me—by imagining you're the kind of person who just—who isn't afraid. Who can just—

PONY: Is this how you imagine the killer?

MARIE: Shh—I'm not gonna hurt you.

PONY: Which one are you right now—which one am I?

MARIE: --.

PONY [*trying out a role*]: I'm the kind of person who isn't afraid.

MARIE: Uh huh.

PONY: I'm—but I see shadows everywhere now.
Except around you—

[*As if he can finally see the depth of these waters . . . Then, this becomes too overwhelming and he panics.*]

PONY: Oh, you know what? I totally forgot that I gotta go.

MARIE: What? No!

PONY: I have a meeting.

MARIE: A meeting? Now?

PONY: Yeah, um, it already started. So, I gotta—do I have everything?

MARIE: I don't understand your schedule!

PONY: I hate to do this [*gives her a quick peck*]—but I'll see you again soon!

MARIE: Pony—

[PONY *fumbles out the door.* MARIE *sits on the edge of her bed, a bit whiplashed. After a moment, she thinks she hears someone entering. But then, nothing. And nothing.*]

MARIE: Hello?

[STELL *comes in.*]

MARIE: Stelly.

STELL: Marie.

MARIE: I wasn't expecting you.

STELL: Who were you expecting?

MARIE: My boyfriend.

STELL: Your boyfriend. Yeah. Night shift?

MARIE: Yeah.

STELL: I want to try.

MARIE: You do.

STELL: What, is that so weird? I want to be a part of it.

MARIE: You think what I do is crazy.

STELL: So you'll do it with him?

MARIE: With who?

STELL: Pony.

MARIE: I haven't.

STELL: You want to.

MARIE: It's different. He's a guy.

STELL: You have a boyfriend.

MARIE: Kind of.

STELL: And Pony is not a boy.

MARIE: I know what he says he is.

STELL: Okay.

MARIE: Does it bother you?

STELL: I want to be your boyfriend.

MARIE: I just want to do my work!

STELL: And you should! I can help.

MARIE: Stell.

STELL: Come on.

MARIE: Okay.
"Do you love me?"

[*A pause as* STELL *registers the beginning of the ritual and contemplates the best response.*]

STELL: "As deep as the ocean."

MARIE: --.
He would never say that.

STELL: He wouldn't?

MARIE: He would be much more brusque. Because at this point he doesn't trust me.

STELL: You?

MARIE: He kills her   me   he kills me, basically. And I am so close, Stell.
I am so close to figuring out how he gets to that point.

STELL: That's dark.

MARIE: You asked.

STELL: Lemme start over.
"I don't love you."

MARIE [*a sigh*]: This isn't gonna work.

STELL: I really want you.

MARIE: It's just—it's what you want.

STELL: Well why can't I ever have that.

[STELL *leaves.*]

MARIE: —Like I am the knife—

[*Sleazy music like "Those Shoes" by the Eagles fades in and plays through the top of the next scene.*]

14. ROADHOUSE

[CAV *in the bar with a drink, looking out.* HEATH *somewhere in the back, wearing sunglasses, keeping watch.* STELL *sits next to* CAV, *who speaks the first line without looking at her.*]

CAV: I hate this bar.

STELL: I know.

CAV: I should really do a study on this.

STELL: Should you?

CAV: These places used to be—well there used to be more of them and they used to be—

STELL: What.

CAV: Huh?

STELL: You trailed off into your nostalgia.

CAV: Oh.

STELL: What places.

CAV: Gay bars. I like to imagine they were community centers. Places of great warmth and acceptance.

STELL: I doubt it.

CAV: They were a home if you got thrown out of yours. Or that's just my fantasy. Have we always been ice queens? You know? Like, like, groups turned in on ourselves, backs to the room. As if we're protecting ourselves from something. From the world. But also . . . from each other.

STELL: Huh.

CAV: I should do a study on how—
I should do a study.

STELL: Or you could enjoy yourself.

CAV: Hm.

[*Neither of them can tonight.*]

CAV: Even after all these years sometimes it's possible to, you know, get affected.

STELL: Yeah?

CAV: I can still remember those first few clients who shook me up.
They were textbook cases and I shivered with every detail that confirmed a diagnosis—I would go to bed with the *DSM-4*'s columns floating in my head.

STELL: What's that?

CAV: A big shrink dictionary about all the kinds of ways to be crazy.

STELL: They say not to read heavy stuff before bed.

CAV: --.

STELL: So what are you saying.
What, do you have—like—feelings? For a client?

CAV: Definitely not!

STELL: So—what?

CAV: --. Stell. What do you see when you look at me.

STELL: --. You're you. What.

CAV: I feel—called into question.

STELL: Why.

CAV: You know how people say, "Things ain't what they used to be?"

STELL: That's what you're saying.

CAV: I feel called into question—as a—butch—person. I mean, what does it mean when someone goes so far beyond—is so far down the gay spectrum, in a sense—that they come back around to the other side and turn into—straight. What does that mean?

STELL: What, now you're not gay enough?

CAV: I mean, it's not a spectrum anymore, it's a carousel!

STELL: Maybe that's where the word "queer" comes from. It kind of sounds like around the circle and off to the side and in the back door or something.

CAV: In some cases. And does that person who comes around the back or comes around, goes beyond the extreme and back to the beginning, is that really the beginning, is that really "straight" or is it some new thing? Like what is it?

STELL: Isn't this your job?

CAV: Is there a word? Or a phrase?

STELL: Overthinking?

CAV: Yeah, forget it.

--.

What's new with you.

STELL: --. She was singing the other day. Tried to play it off like she wasn't. That's the worst—singing. Makes me understand all those orthodox who forbid it! Horrible, horrible—rip your heart out and shred it to bits—

CAV: People don't know what effect they have on other people.

[STELL *takes the stones out of her pocket.*]

STELL: Isn't this pretty—in an ugly kind of way. I like stones.

CAV: Where'd you get those?

STELL: From her.

CAV: Where'd she get 'em?

STELL: From some dude.

CAV: What dude?

STELL: Does it matter?

CAV: We don't really know each other, do we. Who are you again?

STELL: Just a local girl.

CAV: A client stole those off my desk.

STELL: They're just stones.

CAV: Twenty years ago I saved up all my money and I took my partner to Mexico because she had never been out of the country. She had no money. I paid for everything. And she asked me to marry her on the beach. And instead of a ring she gave me a box of stones that she had been keeping since she was little—that she took from a creek as a kid because she knew that one day she'd find someone who didn't care what she was made of.

STELL: Maybe she knew she'd never be made of money. Just dirt from a creek.

CAV: She's gone three years now. I forget what love feels like.

STELL: So do something about it.

CAV: You do something about it.

STELL: Maybe I will.

15. MARIE'S BEDROOM

[MARIE *alone. We finally get to meet her boyfriend—or rather—her "boyfriend." To accomplish this,* MARIE *plays both parts.*]

MARIE: You're back.

BOYFRIEND (MARIE): I brought you some money.

MARIE: That's nice.

BOYFRIEND (MARIE): Are you going to talk to me?

MARIE: We've been through this before.

BOYFRIEND (MARIE): I've been hearing some bad things about you. You've been a bad girl.

MARIE: What do you mean.

BOYFRIEND (MARIE): I mean everyone thinks you're a big tramp.

MARIE: Tramp? Do they still use that word?
What the hell's it mean anyway.

BOYFRIEND (MARIE): It means you're going around flirting with all kinds of people who aren't me.

MARIE: You can't prove that.

BOYFRIEND (MARIE): Why would you need me to prove anything? This isn't court! And I wouldn't need proof if something hadn't happened. I don't have your heart anymore. I can tell.

MARIE: Baby, what can you tell.

BOYFRIEND (MARIE): That you don't look at me the same. You don't want to touch me. I imagine everything I see around here—if I turn it over it's going to be some gift from a lover with little confessions on the underside. I don't want to be around for that.

MARIE: You don't make it easy to be around.

BOYFRIEND (MARIE): After five years you're not so easy yourself.
You want everyone but me because I scare you or something.

MARIE: I don't need your analysis.

BOYFRIEND (MARIE): Then let's call it off.

MARIE: That's fine we can do that.

BOYFRIEND (MARIE): We can call it. We can call it.

MARIE: What's wrong.

BOYFRIEND (MARIE): I'm shit.

MARIE: You're not shit.

BOYFRIEND (MARIE): I'm shit and I don't have a job—shit is a mess. I'm tired of being a guinea pig. I can't do any more medical testing—and they pay me late! What, do they think I have other sources of income after being tied to a hospital bed for weeks? Do they think I don't have a life? Do you think that's why you lost interest? My body pumped with chemicals—did it make me strange.

MARIE: Yeah.

BOYFRIEND (MARIE): If I cut my body do you think I can get them out? I got a knife.

MARIE: Oh please.

BOYFRIEND (MARIE): I want to cut it out. Can you help me?

[*She grabs her own shoulders as he might have.*]

BOYFRIEND (MARIE): Come on!

16. PAY PHONE AT THE ROADHOUSE / NEARBY

PONY: Um, hi Cav, this is Pony. You gave me this number for emergencies. So. I think I'm having one. I. Didn't tell her. That's what we discussed, right? In the middle of it I thought that maybe I could but then I remembered jail. Ha, I remembered jail. I remembered stealing my boss's car and ripping down the thruway so fast I thought I might take off into space! I was driving into oncoming traffic! I was driving down the middle of the road on the yellow line like it was this golden thread to heaven or so I thought despite not believing in heaven. Or hell. Only total blackout. That's what I think happens.

[CAV *in a light, listening to her voicemail. We hear* PONY*'s voice recorded as well as live.*]

The lines between things are curving and when that curve opens up there's the blackout inside. I know that she sits around imagining death and crime and stuff and I can see it in her eyes. I get painted with it. And she has a boyfriend. So. Um. I guess if you hear of any jobs. Let me know. See you next week.

[*Click. Dial tone.* CAV *holds her stones to her heart.*]

17. MARIE'S BEDROOM, CONT'D

MARIE: After he called me a tramp and told me to rip the badness out of him, this is what happened, what he said, what he did.

He said he prays to God but
why won't God blow out the sun?
He got down on his knees and pounded the floor.
He said:
Your hands, I can't feel them anymore.
What would they feel like.
If they touched me.
If you put them on my back.
Just one hand.
Just one finger.
He said:
It used to feel like,
god, like something more
powerful than just a girl
touching me. Like
fast and slow at once. I felt
like gold. I felt like the moon.
Now. I don't feel nothing.
Just ripped at all my fingertips,
water stings my hands.
He said:

While I had the tubes in me today, the lab tech said that this year my birthday was on the Day of Atonement. The most holy day. In his religion. When you're supposed to feel sorry. And fast. And pray. And high on emptiness. So that's tomorrow. The Day of Atonement. Maybe I wanna do it. But then I don't because the last thing I'm being before God is sorry. Someone should apologize to me.

I said I can't listen to this anymore. Stop going on.
He said. The wind.

I said. Go home.
He said. The moon is red.
I said. Leave.
He said. Red. So red.
I said. I said.

18. OUTSIDE THE ROADHOUSE

[*A few moments later.* STELL *exits the bar.* HEATH *follows.*]

HEATH: Stell.

STELL: Are you fucking stalking me?

HEATH: I'm not a stalker.

STELL [*pervy stalker face*]: "I'm not a stalker."

HEATH: You just had a drink with Daddy #1!

STELL: So?

HEATH: You knew them! You could have easily introduced me but instead you put me on this *chase*. I'm paying for your services and I would appreciate some more service!

STELL: Sh! Someone could get the wrong idea. Honey—you gotta give me more to go on if you want to find your man!

HEATH: Do you know what a "man" is?

STELL: You said a father figure! I figured it was metaphoric!

HEATH: If you're fucking with me Stell—

STELL: Are you gonna be a little bitch to the only person who's been nice to you in this town?

HEATH: I'm paying you to be nice.

STELL: --.

HEATH: Who's Daddy #2?

STELL: I'll need the other half.

HEATH: I gave you half up front.

STELL: I ain't your fuckin lawyer, you pay me whether you win or lose.

[HEATH *pulls out the final wad of cash, but holds it a second.*]

HEATH: --.

STELL: What.

HEATH: I just don't want him to hate me.

STELL: --.

HEATH: --.

STELL [*almost tender*]: He wouldn't hate you.

HEATH: --.

STELL: --.

HEATH: He might!

[STELL *puts out her hand.* HEATH *pays her.*]

STELL: Pony.

HEATH [*again, for the sound*]: Pony.

STELL: Lives in the woods back there.

HEATH: Introduce me.

STELL: Can't.

HEATH: We are so done.

STELL: Can I use you as a reference?

19. OUTSIDE THE ROADHOUSE, CONT'D

[CAV *enters.*]

CAV: Stell, is everything alright?

HEATH: We're fine.

STELL: Fine, thank you.
I was just leaving.

[STELL *goes.*]

CAV: So where you headed?

HEATH: To see a friend. How about you?

CAV: Home.

HEATH: Wanna share a cab?

CAV: Do you see any cabs around here?

HEATH: Right.

CAV: I'm hoofin' it.

HEATH: What?

CAV: I'm walking.

HEATH: Oh.

CAV: You got someplace to stay?

HEATH: Sure. Yeah.

CAV: Good.

HEATH: Would you like company, on your walk?

CAV: No, I'll be fine.

HEATH: You seem very familiar. I feel like I know you. Do you think we could be related?

CAV: Yeah. I think we met on the bus.

HEATH: That's not what I meant. Like, family. Do you think we could be related like family?

CAV: I don't have any family.

HEATH: Everybody has family.

CAV: Look I gotta go. Do you need money?

HEATH: I'll be fine.

CAV: Oh right.

HEATH: My name's Heath.

CAV: I remember.

HEATH: What's your name?

CAV: --. Cav.

HEATH: Is that short for something?

CAV: Leave me alone, kid.

HEATH: Look, I hate that I'm even asking. But I'm trying to find someone important. Is Cav your original name?

CAV: Is Heath your original name?

HEATH: Fine.

CAV: I gotta go.
You should too.
Back to wherever you came from.
I'm not related to you.

[CAV *goes.*]

HEATH: --.
--.
--.
Liar.

[HEATH *throws something, kicks something. Sits down on his pack.*]

HEATH: Pony.

20. IN THE WOODS BETWEEN PONY'S HOUSE AND MARIE'S HOUSE

[HEATH *sleeping at the side of the path.* MARIE *enters. She looks terrible, some combination of beaten, distraught, and dragged through the dirt.*]

MARIE: You can't sleep here—

HEATH: Fuck off.

MARIE: —but I'm going to try.

HEATH: Hey lady, what are you doing?

MARIE: Shhhh—it's time to sleep.

HEATH: But I'm a strange man sleeping on the ground in the woods. You don't know me.

MARIE: Yeah, yeah.

HEATH: Oh my god, what happened to you?

MARIE: Nothing. Shhhh—

HEATH: Who did this to you? Do you know? We can get the police. Was it your boyfriend?

MARIE: My "boyfriend."

HEATH: Was it?

MARIE [*of his cheek*]: I like your fuzz.

HEATH: Who are you?

MARIE: Marie.

HEATH: Marie, don't go to sleep. It's time to wake up, okay? We're going to get you some help.

MARIE: I'm going to my friend's house.

HEATH: Oh yeah? Who's that?

MARIE: Pony.

HEATH: Oh really? Why don't I take you there. And Pony can help you get cleaned up and we can take you to a doctor.

MARIE: No doctors.

HEATH: But you're all bloody. Don't you want to be clean?

MARIE: I know I sound drunk. I sound like a drunk sorority girl. I'm hearing my voice in my head. I'm sorry. You're a good guy. I'm just gonna walk over there.

HEATH: Whoa—steady—let me help you.

MARIE: Yeah maybe. But just so you know, I'm not drunk.

HEATH: I know.

MARIE: I'm very intelligent and I got in a fight. And it's complicated. And he got mad at me. And I gotta finish my research. I'm in the middle of research.

HEATH: What are you researching?

MARIE: Murder.

HEATH: Oh.

MARIE: Yeah. There was a murder here. A guy killed his girlfriend. Right over there actually. By that creek. Stabbed her to death. He's in custody now. Gonna be hanged.

HEATH: Are you talking to his friends and the cops or something?

MARIE: Did that. Now I'm reading about existentialism.

HEATH: Oh.

MARIE: Yeah, it's more theoretical, what I'm doing. Mostly I'm reading the newspapers and seeing how people are writing about this. And what it does to fear. People's fear around here. Because there's crime here, you know. You really shouldn't sleep outside. This isn't—a bourgeois weekend destination.

HEATH: I know.

MARIE: Not that everybody's violent—but you never know.

HEATH: Right.

MARIE: Pony's house is right there.

HEATH: Can I come with you? I'd like to meet him.

MARIE: Maybe it's better if you don't.

HEATH: Why?

MARIE: He and I have things to discuss.

HEATH: I can just wait outside and when you're done discussing things maybe I can come in and meet him.

MARIE: I don't think there's going to be time for that.

HEATH: I won't take any time.

MARIE: You. Sleep. Good boy.

HEATH: I'll just. Wait outside. If you need to go to the hospital.

[*She's gone.*]

HEATH: Whoa.

21. PONY'S HOUSE

[PONY *at the door.* MARIE *falling into his arms, collapsing.*]

PONY: Did he hurt you?

MARIE: Hi Pony.

PONY: Does he know you're here?

MARIE: You're the only one who knows.

PONY: Good. Oh boy.

MARIE: And I called Stell.

PONY: Oh great.

MARIE: You don't like Stell?

PONY: She's—devoted?

MARIE: You should have seen her ice skate.

PONY: Really.

MARIE: Backwards, forwards, little jumps.

[PONY *tries to brush her hair off a scrape—*]

MARIE: Ow—

PONY: Sorry.

MARIE: Naptime—

PONY: Marie, you have to keep talking so you don't die.

MARIE: I don't wanna talk politics.

PONY: No pressure.

MARIE: I met your neighbor.

PONY: I don't have a neighbor.

MARIE: He's waiting outside.

PONY: My neighbor?

MARIE: You don't have a neighbor.

PONY: What happened to you? Did you do something?

MARIE: --.

PONY: --.

MARIE: --.

PONY: Well?

MARIE: Don't worry about it. --.

PONY: Oh boy.

MARIE: I'm gonna rest my eyes.

PONY: No—don't—hey wait—

[She's passed out. He watches her. And watches her.]

22. PONY'S HOUSE, FIVE MINUTES LATER

[There's a knock. STELL *is there.]*

STELL: What did you do.

[She rushes over to the passed-out MARIE.*]*

Oh baby. [*To* PONY] Could you cover her up or something?

PONY: What are you doing here.

STELL: She wasn't home. So I took a wild guess.
I told you not to get involved.

PONY: Because you wanted her to show up on your doorstep?

STELL: Threatening me is not a good idea.

PONY: Where was the threat? That wasn't a threat.

STELL: You're in over your head.

PONY: I can see that this is totally fucked up but Marie and I can handle it without you. Isn't it messier if you're involved?

STELL: No because I'm pretty sure you were responsible for this.

PONY: What?!

STELL: Giving her gifts?

PONY: I didn't—

STELL: Those stones? The guy is insane!

PONY: So you let her stay with him all these years and now you want to blame me? You're totally in love with her and she kisses me in the shadows at the fair and everything that ever happened is my fault? What have you been doing? Pining away while she gets beat up once a week? She does, doesn't she?

STELL: Can you get me some water and a cloth please? I'm going to clean her up.

PONY: --.

STELL: You should be feeling responsible. You should be cleaning this up. You should be giving her money to get the hell out of here.

PONY: I don't have any money!

STELL: Bet you don't.

[PONY *brings a rag and water.*]

PONY: Here.

STELL: You can leave us alone now. You can go.

PONY: I live here.

STELL: There is no "Marie and you." You're just a placeholder.
A dummy. A prop. For her research.

PONY: That's not true. [*Whispering*] Isn't her research kind of bullshit?

STELL [*terrifyingly*]: Go. [*To Marie, saccharine*] Sweetie.

PONY: Jesus!

[PONY *storms out. He and* HEATH *are on opposite sides of the house, can't see each other.*]

23. PONY'S HOUSE, CONT'D

[STELL *alone with* MARIE, *who shows no signs of hearing.*]

STELL: Do you want me to carve your skin with marks to remember this?
Should I mark myself?
Why do I have to carry you inside me all the time?
Why do I have to know all about you
like when you want things
and what you eat and
still have to take care of myself too?
Maybe the wind can come
and rip off the roof of this cabin
and take my soul away
and fly to the devil
and the devil can come
and eat my mind
and I can disappear with you.
Then.
My hair will be blown.
You'll wear a dress.
All the stupid men will melt
and we can walk north.

[*She holds, reverently, for a moment. Has an idea, like remembering the location of a misplaced thing. She homes in. She finds where* PONY *has hidden his only money in the world. A few bills in that beat-up tin. She pockets the money. Well, almost all of it. Okay, all of it. She curls up beside* MARIE.]

24. OUTSIDE PONY'S HOUSE

[*Night.* PONY, *who let* MARIE *(and* STELL*) have the bed, is sleeping outside.* MARIE *finally wakes. She comes out of the house, wrapped in a sheet, and sits on top of* PONY.]

MARIE: Pony.

PONY: What.

MARIE: You brought me here?

PONY: It's a long story.

MARIE: What happened.

PONY: I was going to ask you that.

MARIE: It's like my body knows but my mind doesn't.

PONY: Yeah?

MARIE: Do you think it's dangerous for me to be here?

PONY: You're safe now.

[MARIE *brings her mouth to his. It's not a kiss but it's not chaste. Like she's transmitting information. Telling his body what to do. She approximates some of the movement she describes on* PONY*'s body.*]

MARIE: I had your stones in my hand.

[*She drops the sheet she was holding to cover her body. She brings* PONY'S *hand to her skin.*]

I wanted to put them inside me. I held them against me. I thought of you. But you weren't there. You weren't there. But then he was there and he saw that. He couldn't have known what I was thinking.

[*She tries to take* PONY*'s shirt off.*]

PONY [*in a whisper, meant to deflect attention*]: No.

MARIE: --. He had just come back from one of the medical tests he does to make money. Sometimes it takes us some adjusting time to get back into our thing.
So I tried to hug him.
He pushed me away.

[*She pushes* PONY*'s hands away.*]

Just for a second and then he lunged.

[*She pins his shoulders to the ground.*]

I was scared and it was like he had a thousand weapons and a thousand arms and had let in a whole army or something. He raised his arm and I thought he had a knife, and a gun, and a fist, and a stick. I thought he was going to just slash my face quickly and in one sharp tear it would be over. But he was all over me like sex again with his hands around my neck.

[*She tries to put her hands around* PONY*'s neck but he rolls her over and pins her. She tries to pull his head down to her face.*]

He wanted to cry and crush his cheek into mine to see if I would love him and I did. Feel tender. And I remembered that once sex like this was what I wanted. Rough. I rolled him over and pinned him. Then he pinned me and I got my knee in his groin and he howled and hit me.

[PONY *tries to untangle himself from this. Tries to get them sitting apart—he can only get her out from under him—she won't let him go.*]

Then I had a thousand weapons. I had guns and knives. I took my knife.

[*She raises a fist.*]

He took his knife.

[*She makes* PONY'*s hand into a fist and raises it.* PONY *lets it fall.*]

No, like this.

[*She adjusts* PONY'*s hand.* PONY *is not into it.*]

Like this.

[*Adjustment.*]

Like this.

[*Finally. Both have fists raised as if they held knives. And hold. Hold.*]

[MARIE *lets her fist relax.* PONY *does too.* MARIE *reaches for* PONY'*s shirt again. He brushes her away.*]

MARIE: I'm not allowed to touch you, am I.

PONY: No.

MARIE: Why.

PONY: --.

MARIE: Keep your hand up.

PONY: Why are you telling me this.

MARIE: Do it!

PONY: No!

[*They struggle:* MARIE *trying to grab his hands and make them into fists,* PONY *trying to still her wild arms. He succeeds in holding her arms down; he holds her from behind. Hard. She lets him, it helps her finish:*]

MARIE: And I don't know what was next. Maybe there was a great sound like wasps. Maybe it was a gasping for air like getting pushed to the ground. Maybe he fucked me until I shut down. Maybe I pressed my hands into his face until it shattered.

[PONY *tightens his grip, and* MARIE *inhales sharply in response.*]

PONY: Why did you come here.

MARIE: Why did you come here—why did you move here at all—why did you talk to me—why won't you tell me anything—let me touch you.

PONY: Here, tonight, why come to my house?

MARIE: I need you.

PONY: Do you even see me?

[MARIE *makes contact with* PONY *slowly, carefully, in a way that he's not ready for, but in a way that shows him that she wants him exactly as he really is.*

In prior drafts I had MARIE *unbutton* PONY*'s shirt, revealing his bound chest. It was a kind of slow-moving assault, punctuated by* MARIE*'s intense gaze.* PONY *looked like it made him want to vomit from fear and self-loathing.*

Because this play is meant to subvert gendered violence, not replicate it, PONY*'s body shall not be revealed. Our bodies do not define our gender.*]

[*The rest of* MARIE*'s story:*]

MARIE: We must have really hurt each other.
We both passed out.
At one point I think we took our clothes off.
And then I came here.

[MARIE *releases* PONY *from the position. He gives her a look that says, "I wasn't ready for that." He breathes.*

He sits apart from her.

She wants to connect but doesn't know how.

He won't look at her.

MARIE *doesn't have the capacity to figure this out right now.*

She goes back in the house to go to bed.]

25. OUTSIDE AND INSIDE PONY'S HOUSE

[*The next morning.* PONY *asleep outside.*

HEATH *is shaking* PONY *awake.*]

HEATH: Hey.

PONY: Huh? Whoa.

HEATH: It's okay, it's okay.

PONY: Do I know you?

HEATH: I'm Heath.

PONY: Good morning?

HEATH: Don't worry, the women are gone.

PONY: What? Did you just say—
They're gone?!

[*He's up, he's bolting inside the house, he's looking all around for them. He's looking out the other side, out all the windows. Looking under the bed.*]

PONY: How could they be gone! What the fuck what the fuck what the fuck. Oh my god. Did you see them go?

HEATH: No—

PONY: But you knew they were here.

HEATH: I was sleeping on the side of the road—

PONY: Not recommended.

HEATH: —and I saw Marie go in.

PONY: Marie.

HEATH: She wouldn't let me come in with her. She told me to go to sleep. And I was so tired that I did.

PONY: Did you see Stell?

HEATH: Stell was here?

PONY: You know Stell?

HEATH: She's my—she's the only person I really know up here.

PONY: What the hell are you doing here then.

HEATH: Trying to meet you.

PONY: Me?

HEATH: Yeah.

PONY: Why? Look around. I live in—pretty much a shack, okay? I have no money—

[*A light bulb. He darts for his money tin hiding place—whatever was there is now gone.*]

[*In falsetto*] Holy fucking shit! They took my fucking money!

[*He throws the tin on the ground.*]

This is kind of a bad time. For guests. I think maybe you should go.

HEATH: Wait but I have to—

[PONY *pulls* HEATH *up by his collar, trying to shove him out.*]

PONY: I need to be alone.

HEATH: But—

PONY: Please just go. And don't sleep outside my house you fucking weirdo! Oh my god.

HEATH: Pony, I want to be here for you.

[PONY *recklessly slams around his room.*]

PONY: Well that's not what I want though that doesn't seem to matter.

HEATH: I'm related to you.

PONY: Obviously I'm a big fucking chump. I'm a fucking pawn in that game. I don't even know if she was for real about me!

HEATH: Stell isn't for real about anything.

PONY: You do fucking know her, don't you. But I think I know the one thing she is for real about.

HEATH: Marie?

PONY: Yeah.

HEATH: Pony, I'm your sister's kid.

[*Hold.*]

PONY: What?

[*Hold.*]

HEATH: Don't hate me.

PONY: Why would I hate you?

HEATH: --.

PONY: You transitioned.

HEATH: We haven't seen each other in a long time. Since I was little I think.

PONY: I didn't think she—I didn't think you guys knew I went by Pony.

HEATH: I do now. And I like it.

PONY: Thanks.

HEATH: Heath.

PONY: Yeah. Thanks, Heath.

HEATH: I wanted to meet you really bad.

PONY: Well. You did. So.

HEATH: How's it going?

PONY: You mean up here? In this shack? Or with these fucking inmates at the insane asylum of this town. Awesome.

HEATH: You look good.

PONY: Does your mom call you Heath?

HEATH: She's gotten used to it.

PONY: That's good.

HEATH: She's still working on you though.

PONY: What did she tell you, how did you know—about me.

HEATH: Heard things.

PONY [*for the sound of it*]: Heath.

HEATH: I need a father.

PONY: Whoaaaa, um—

HEATH: I do—I need—

PONY: It's—impossible. I'm too busy.

HEATH: Look, I know that I don't know everything about the world.

PONY: You're freakin' me out.

HEATH: Let me live with you.

PONY: Oh. Um—

HEATH: Please.

PONY: —there's not really any room.

HEATH: We can get a bigger house. My mom will help us.

PONY: She will?

HEATH: Pony, we're family.

PONY: But, but, being with you would—give me away.

[HEATH *takes that in.*]

HEATH: It doesn't have to be like that.

PONY: But it is.

HEATH: You can—be out.

PONY: It's not safe.

HEATH: Look—I don't understand this place—but we can go where we know it's safe. South City—

PONY: I can't go back there.

HEATH: You think it's fancy boutiques and yoga and it is, sure, part of it. But there are restaurants and parks and just regular places where no one gives a shit, okay? Nobody cares. And you can kiss your person in public and hold their hand and it doesn't fucking matter because everyone's kissing their person and holding hands and who gives a shit about you and your ambiguity—you can just—be a speck.

PONY: You sound like a commercial.

HEATH: Okay. Or else not a city—there are other country places too! I'm sure! Just not with those lugnuts on the other side of the woods.

PONY: See—what am I gonna show you.

HEATH: Everything else.

PONY: How do you know?

HEATH: It was hiding that almost killed me.
It was the silence—

PONY: I'm sorry, I can't.

HEATH: Pony—

PONY: I just can't.

26. INSIDE A GREASY SPOON WAY NORTH

[*Daybreak elsewhere, the same morning, very far north.* STELL *and* MARIE *on the road.* MARIE *is heartbroken, shell-shocked.* STELL *has* PONY*'s money.*]

STELL: You want coffee?

MARIE: Where are we?

STELL: North.

MARIE: Where's Pony?

STELL: Here eat this.

MARIE: --.

STELL: You know, there's a waterfall near here. We can go see it. People say it's like God.

MARIE: There's something—around here—all these international tourists—all the stores looked so depressed—like mouths without teeth—like everything's a front—or a brothel—or a meth lab.

STELL: That's depressing. We're just on a trip. We should enjoy it. Like a vacation.

MARIE: I've never been to one.

STELL: A vacation?

MARIE: A brothel.

STELL: Oh.

MARIE: I should look into that.

STELL: We're going to stay in a hotel.

MARIE: Really?

STELL: Pony gave us some money.

MARIE: He did? That's so nice.

STELL: We all talked and decided it would be best if you and I went away for a little bit.

MARIE: Do you think I'll lose my job?

STELL: You can call in.

MARIE: What happened to my boyfriend?

STELL: I don't know.

MARIE: Does he know we left?

STELL: Marie, he almost killed you.

MARIE: I don't know what I did to him.

STELL: Did you kill him.

MARIE: I don't know.

[MARIE *turns away. She turns back, sees* STELL *watching. Turns away again.*]

27. SOCIAL SERVICES OFFICE

[PONY *waits. Finally,* CAV *enters. It is awkward.*]

PONY: Busy today.

CAV: That's why I came all the way out here. Normally I'm just here for counseling. Didn't want you to have to deal with the front desk.

PONY: I sounded real bad on that voicemail, huh.

CAV: Like you could use someone to talk to.

PONY: Hm.

CAV: Do you want to? Talk?

PONY [*A beat, then*]: So how does this work.

CAV: These are the welfare forms. You gotta fill them out. And we need either a document from this column and a document from this column or just this document here. Got it? Either column A *and* column B or just column C.
You got those?

PONY: I—I don't have any of those.

CAV: What about pieces of mail. An electric bill? Gas bill? We can take anything with your address on it.

PONY: I got 'em at home. I could bring 'em back.

CAV: Okay. So you fill this thing out—ever been arrested, list some references—and I can get your paperwork started right away. Just—when you come back, bring twenty dollars, the clinic charges a fee.

PONY: A fee?

CAV: Yeah, it's twenty dollars to register if you don't have the proper documents. It's an administrative fee that covers—

PONY: How come all the other times—

CAV: That was counseling and the study. This is registration.

PONY: I don't have twenty dollars. I don't have—anything.

CAV: I'm so sorry.

PONY: Maybe I shouldn't have come.

CAV: No, no. You did the right thing by coming in today. This was the first step.

PONY: I guess. First step to what.

CAV: Getting your life back.

PONY: Sometimes—

Sometimes I think I have bad blood. Like there's something inside me and I don't know what I could do if I ever lost control of myself—maybe something bad. And so far, like I've lived for a while, right, and I haven't done anything that bad and I'm afraid if I really don't have any money that all the bad things I ever thought of—I won't have anything to lose. Are you going to put that in my file?

CAV: --.

PONY: Look. I'm sorry I don't have twenty dollars.

CAV: That door right there leads to the alley.

PONY: You kicking me out?

CAV: No. --.

PONY: I can—just go?

CAV: I didn't say that.

PONY: But you just said—

CAV: --.

PONY: This a trap? You got police out there?

CAV: There's about one cop in this town and since it's happy hour you can guess where he is right now.

PONY: Right. Well. Thanks.

CAV: See you later Pony—with those documents?

PONY: Yeah.

[PONY *leaves out the back. Beat.*]

28. SEVERAL PLACES AT ONCE

[CAV *takes a twenty out of her own wallet and clips it to* PONY*'s file.* PONY *bursts out the back door of the center.*

MARIE *speaks from a dream:*]

MARIE: Should I rip out the sky's throat?
Where do you think I got those stones.

Tore 'em out to save the sky from choking.
I asked it: How much breath should I let you keep?
I asked it over and over. How much?
What's the little little tiniest that you need to clear the fever?
It said, rip out these stones.
It said, clear my pipes!
It said: I weigh a hundred million tons!
You don't know it but the earth sits inside me like this stone in my throat
and I need you to get it out!
Get it out!

[CAV *slams the files down on her desk.*
PONY *gasps for air in the alley.*
MARIE *bolts upright and gasps for air.*
STELL *sleeps beside her in the hotel room.*
STELL *wakes up and notices* MARIE.]

STELL: What is it.

MARIE: Nothing.

[HEATH *inside* PONY*'s house—he spins around really fast till he's dizzy and almost falls.*]

29. OUTSIDE THE SOCIAL SERVICES CENTER

[CAV *runs out the back door.*]

CAV: Hey! Pony!

PONY: What.

CAV: Pony, come back.

PONY: What do you want.

CAV: To talk. I can see that you're angry.

PONY: Because you're following me.

CAV: I'm not following you.

PONY: You're running behind me.

CAV: Okay I'll stop. I'm not following you.

[CAV *stops.* PONY *keeps going.*]

CAV: Hey. Get back here!

PONY: See, now you're doing it again!

CAV: Hey, please come back.

PONY: I gotta be somewhere.

CAV: Where are you going?

PONY: None of your business.

CAV: I just didn't want you to leave angry.

PONY: Are we having therapy outside the office now? I thought you were the tax collector.

CAV: Pony—

PONY: I'm sick of this shit.

CAV: I'm sorry.

PONY: Why's it gotta cost money to get help! Shouldn't that be free?

CAV: It's horrible.

PONY: Yeah.

CAV: Are you going to meet Marie?

[*This stops* PONY.]

PONY: Stop fucking asking me things!

CAV: --.

[PONY *starts to crumble.*]

I'm having a problem not crossing the line here.

PONY: What line.

CAV: Patient and friend.

PONY: I'm not your fucking patient and I'm not your fucking friend.

CAV: --.

PONY: --.

CAV: Fine.

PONY: I'm just done. That was harsh. I'm sorry.

CAV: Maybe you could just tell me—

PONY: What.

CAV: Could—could I pass?

PONY: What?!

CAV: As a man. Could. I pass.

PONY: --.
Maybe.

CAV: Pony—

PONY: Is the whole world going to sell me out?

CAV: I'm not.

PONY: What do you know.

30. MARIE AND STELL IN A MOTEL ROOM

[MARIE *regains her lucidity throughout.*]

MARIE: Stell.

STELL: I didn't say anything.

MARIE: Stell, I know what you're doing.

STELL: Getting dressed?

MARIE: Not that.

STELL: Taking you on the ride of your life?
You hungry?

MARIE: Why we're here.

STELL: I'm saving your ass, baby.

MARIE: I know.

STELL: Can't argue with the detective.

MARIE: --. Come here.

STELL: What.

MARIE: Come closer.
You are trying to save me, aren't you.

STELL: Yeah.

MARIE: You love me so much.

STELL: Yeah.

MARIE: You want me to have a good life.

STELL: Yeah.

MARIE: And you want to be with me.

STELL: That's right.

MARIE: So you figured out a way and you took me out of there.

STELL: Those woods were bad for us.

MARIE: There was violence.

STELL: And distractions.

MARIE: Distractions?

STELL: From just being together.

MARIE: Oh yeah. So you arranged this.

STELL: When I saw how upset you were getting—

MARIE: With the research—

STELL: And with Pony, how he was getting in your way.

MARIE: Oh.

STELL: Because I care about you and I want you to just—

MARIE: What.

STELL: Just be happy.

MARIE: Mm.

STELL: That's it. Just be happy.

MARIE: Be happy with you.

STELL: Yeah.

MARIE: You care so much about me.

STELL: Yeah.

MARIE: --. So you took Pony's money. And that boy's money.

STELL: What? No.

MARIE: --.

STELL: Pony gave us money—he knew the woods were bad for you. You were scaring him.

MARIE: Did he tell you that?

STELL: In confidence.

MARIE: I see.

STELL: I'm the only one who cares enough to stay with you. I'm the only one.

MARIE: Pony—

STELL: Pony thinks you're crazy.

MARIE: He said that?

STELL: They all do, Marie. You need a fresh start.

MARIE: --.

STELL: --.

MARIE: I'm gonna—I'm gonna take a walk.

STELL: You can't do that.

MARIE: Where'm I gonna go?

STELL: --.

MARIE: Think I'm gonna leave you? Here all alone in Canada?

STELL: There's nothing back there for you.

MARIE: I just need a little air.

STELL: Marie.

MARIE: Watch the TV.

STELL: It's hot when you tell me what to do.

[*Sound of TV—an '80s music video. Something like Taylor Dayne's "Tell It to My Heart."*]

MARIE: I'll be right back.

[MARIE *exits.*]

31. RIVER BANK

PONY: The edge of the water.
The earth has boundaries so why don't I.
My skin ends here but it's no protection,
other peoples' passions carving out a canyon—as if—
I'm made of clay,
A void,
The screen they shine their movie on
for a story no one knows.
Or a story known too well.

32. PONY'S HOUSE

[HEATH *alone.* CAV *enters with a paper shopping bag, which she sets down.*]

CAV: Hey. Where's Pony?

HEATH: He's not here.

CAV: Then why are you.

HEATH: I belong here.

CAV: I'm a—friend.

HEATH: Why don't I believe you.

CAV: Look kid—I just need to talk to him.

HEATH: I told you he's not here.

CAV: We might need to work together.

HEATH: Why.

CAV: He might be—upset.

HEATH: Did you—upset him?

CAV: No. It's just. Some upsetting things might be going on.

HEATH: I can see that.

CAV: Not me. Him.

HEATH: I know all about it.

CAV: Then you're gonna wanna be nice.

HEATH: I'm plenty fucking nice.

CAV: I haven't done anything to you.

HEATH: You've been a complete asshole.

CAV: Oh that's mature.

HEATH: Watch out—it's extremely childish in here—plus with the testosterone—this is no place for old stone butches.

[CAV *is fast. She grabs* HEATH *by the neck.*]

CAV: Shut up you little fuck.

HEATH: Good! Beat the shit out of me! Show me who's boss!

CAV: Shut your fucking mouth.

HEATH: Ow! Come on! Put the little tranny in his place!*

[CAV *sees* HEATH *struggling for breath and, disgusted with herself, drops him.* HEATH *falls on the floor, tries to recover.*]

CAV: You. Have no idea. How hard we fought. How hard they fought before us. And for this? For this?

[CAV *turns away.* STELL *enters. She looks bad.*]

STELL: What's going on? Hey Cavvie. Hey kid.

[STELL *can feel the tension in the room and now it's directed at her. She starts to back toward the door.* HEATH *knows that* PONY'*s money is missing because of the women;* CAV *is bluffing her way through, taking cues from* HEATH, *though she suspects the same.*]

HEATH: Hey Stell. Where you been?

CAV: Yeah, where you been?

STELL: Long weekend.

HEATH: It's Thursday.

STELL: Find your daddy yet?

HEATH: Pony wants his money back.

STELL: Well why don't you give it to him.

---

*Productions may choose to replace the slur in this line with a differently charged alternative, such as "freak." Consultation with cast, crew, and community recommended.

HEATH: I didn't take his money. You did.

STELL: Why would I take Pony's money. Does he even have any money?

HEATH: Oh stop—you have no moral code.

CAV: Stell, where did you go for the weekend?

STELL: Oh you know, up north.

CAV: Oh. Where?

STELL: The Falls.

CAV: Oh real nice up there.

STELL: Yeah real nice. Lots of tourists though.

CAV: Yeah. Who did you go with?

STELL: Marie.

CAV: Oh. That's awfully nice.

STELL: We had a good time.

CAV: Where is she now?

STELL: Oh she's unpacking at her place.

CAV: How's she doing?

STELL: Relaxed.

[*She sees* CAV *and* HEATH *exchange a look and knows she's in trouble.*]

I think I'm gonna go. See you guys later.

[STELL *darts for the door.* CAV *and* HEATH *pounce to keep her inside.*]

What are you guys gonna do—little sexual violence to spice things up? 'Cause that'd be cute.

HEATH: Ew.

STELL: I already gave you what you wanted.

HEATH: Don't lie.

STELL: What, these people aren't good enough for you?

CAV: Did you hurt Marie?

STELL: Cav. This is stupid. You guys need to calm down.

HEATH [*to* STELL]: I want my money back.

CAV [*to* HEATH]: I thought we were talking about Pony's money.

STELL [*to* HEATH]: I don't know what you're talking about.

CAV [*to* HEATH]: What are you talking about.

HEATH [*a decision not to make this public*]: Nothing.

[HEATH *lets* STELL *go, roughly.*]

CAV [*to* HEATH]: What was that.

STELL: It's nothing, Cav.

CAV: Nothing?

HEATH: Nothing!

[CAV *and* STELL *pause.*]

Both of you: out.

STELL: I can't help it if Pony doesn't want you, Heath.

[STELL *goes.* CAV *is still there. A staredown. Then:*]

HEATH: If you don't have anything nice to say—

[*This hangs for a second. Then,* CAV *crosses to the door and picks up her paper bag. Is she about to leave? She is unsure.*]

CAV: I just wanted to see if he needed anything.
Like maybe some food. I went to the market.
I have bread and milk. And meat and honey.
And greens. Lemons. Sweet peas.
I could cook. I don't cook very well.
I cook well enough. I cook basic things.
Or one thing at a time.
I feed myself. I can just double it.
Or triple it. Sometimes I do that anyway
if I want to make a lot of food.
If I want to make it last.
Food is expensive.
So I thought. I could help.
And he's probably stressed out.
And it's nice to have someone
to cook for you.
To cook for.

[HEATH *relents, takes his own space, and gives no response.* CAV *stands at the door.*]

33. RIVER BANK, CONT'D

[PONY *throwing stones. Hard. Throwing his whole body, almost. Almost into the river.*]

MARIE: Careful.

[PONY *whips around to see her.*]

MARIE: I came back.

PONY: Why.

MARIE: Aren't you glad to see me?

PONY: No.

MARIE: Pony.

PONY: You don't care about me.

MARIE: That's not true.

PONY: You're plugging me into your fake detective shit.

MARIE: I'm sharing my life with you.

PONY: It's bullshit!

MARIE: It's not.

PONY: It's shit, Marie! I don't want it!

MARIE: Why are you being so mean?

PONY: You stole all my money!

MARIE: What?

PONY: You and Stell. You took everything.

MARIE: Stell told me you gave it to us. To escape. So my boyfriend wouldn't follow us.

PONY: Well he didn't chase you here.

MARIE: That's a relief.

PONY: I mean—does he even exist?

MARIE: It's over with him.

PONY: Oh! Too bad we never met! Don't you got a picture?

MARIE: I'm gonna show you a picture? No way!

PONY: Come on—it's an elaborate scam—you totally have a picture.

MARIE: It's not a scam!

PONY: Then show me a picture!

MARIE: FINE.

[*She pulls one out.*]

PONY: Oh he's cute.

MARIE: Yeah.

PONY: Really handsome.

MARIE: Mm.

PONY: That's George Clooney!*

MARIE: --.

PONY: In the role of a lifetime!

MARIE: --.

PONY: You must think I'm a fucking moron.

MARIE: No.

PONY: So if anybody asks to see a picture of your boyfriend you're going to show them a picture of George Clooney? This whole time he's in your wallet?

MARIE: Yeah—

*Update with relevant nontoxic cis-male dramatic lead or good-guy action hero, one who reads about ten years older than the actor playing Marie. Should skew toward smoldering.

PONY: Now—if I had to cast an abusive boyfriend—it wouldn't be him!

MARIE: I guess.

PONY: And you thought I wouldn't recognize him?

MARIE: He's sympathetic—

PONY: Where's Stell?

MARIE: Aren't you glad I came back?

PONY: What more do you want from me?

MARIE: Pony, I solved the crime.

PONY: I don't want to hear any more of that sad tale.

MARIE: But Pony, I think it's a story about us.

PONY: It's a messed-up story, is what it is.

MARIE: Hold on—

PONY: No, I know what this is. Since you know all about me—now that you know my secret—I'm a very complex character. The character with something to hide.

MARIE: I'm not gonna use you like that.

PONY: Oh I'm so curious, how are you gonna use me then? Come on Marie, everybody knows that at the end you have to kill the queer.

MARIE: Stop it!

PONY: I've been revealed as not truly a man but someone who was actually born as a woman and is now deceiving the world in the shape of—let's face it—the devil—and now that the deceived woman has learned my secret and had no choice but to run off with my worldly possessions with her "best friend," she's come back to give me what I deserve.

MARIE: You're twisting everything.

PONY: No—wait! If she's not here to kill me that must mean that in this story—I'm supposed to kill myself! That's what happens to bad queers, Marie. Lynching, murder, or suicide. There's really no other narrative out. So which is it.

MARIE: Pony.

PONY: I don't see anyone else here. So it's all up to you and me.

MARIE: --.

PONY: What are you in the mood for?

MARIE: --.

PONY: To be honest, I don't really want to die.

MARIE: --. The queers never do.

PONY: Right. That's why we have to kill them.

MARIE: Well I don't want to die!

PONY: Marie—

MARIE: And you're not the only one who's queer!

PONY: Good!

MARIE: But Pony, maybe—

PONY: What.

MARIE: —nobody has to die.

PONY: --.

MARIE: --.

PONY: --. I thought that's all you cared about.

MARIE: What.

PONY: Death. Danger. Destruction. Your whole investigation.

MARIE: I'm working through something.

PONY: Yeah Marie but what is it, because it fucking scares me.

MARIE: About how a person could be so desperate, get to this point, so twisted, could believe, could feel this violence as the only way.

I think it's like, it must seem like he has a right, or like she's an extension of himself. Or like—consensual. Oh my god what if it seems consensual.

PONY: What? Whoa.

MARIE: And that's what's in his mind. It's like everybody agrees. Like the victim, like the town, like the earth and sky and God. That poor people are worthless. So there's nothing saying why not.

PONY: But did you have to make me go through it?

MARIE: --.

PONY: For a minute there I thought you thought I was that guy.

MARIE: Oh, what did I do.

PONY: You almost ripped me open.

MARIE: I—. Pony, I'm sorry.

PONY: That might not be enough.

MARIE: Well I'm not running.

[PONY *wants to believe her.*]

[STELL *appears upstage, watching.*]

[CAV *and* HEATH *sit tensely at* PONY*'s house.*]

CAV: What kind of story is this?

HEATH: It's an action thriller soap opera mystery.

CAV: Am I supposed to understand that?

[*They quietly bicker under the transition to the river:*

HEATH: You could open your mind to the possibility that—

CAV: —My mind has opened far enough!

HEATH: Ugh, do you even have friends?

Continue ad libbing if needed. They begin to resemble family.]

[*Until, at the river:*]

MARIE: Tell me.

PONY: I don't have the words.

[*We catch a glimpse of* STELL *walking away.*]

[PONY *and* MARIE *focus on each other.*]

MARIE: I think you do.

[*He does.*]

PONY: I'm shaking.

[PONY *faces out, his focus growing deeper. He thinks about what he might do next.*]

THE OTHER SIDE OF THE FOREST

Pony, Transmasculinity, and Generational Shift

Miriam Felton-Dansky

Toward the end of Sylvan Oswald's *Pony*, its title character agonizes over the narrative structure of his own life. Pony is transmasculine and passing, formerly incarcerated, and a recent arrival to a depressed upstate New York town. Can a trans narrative, he asks, ever be more than a tale of violence and erasure? Reflecting Oswald's frequent use of self-reflexive dramaturgies as strategies for individual and societal self-examination, the scene pushes against the bounds of expected storytelling, demanding to know if a trans character can live in a non-tragic mode, inhabit a paradigm other than the doomed quest for survival. "That's what happens to bad queers, Marie," Pony says to his lover. "Lynching, murder, or suicide. There's really no other narrative out."[1]

Marie, though, resists this fatalism, and so does the play. *Pony*—begun in 2005, with a 2011 world premiere and new productions featuring revised text in 2022—offers a dramatic structure built to encompass multiple trans narratives and an expansive landscape that includes queer elders and trans youth, romantic love and intergenerational longing. An epic story that holds dialogue with Georg Büchner's explosive, fragmentary 1837 play *Woyzeck* and with decades of queer and trans communal conversation, Oswald's drama follows Pony to an unnamed town "on the other side of the forest from *Woyzeck*," where he tries to start again. Alongside him, queer life unfolds, as the play introduces a constellation of queer and trans characters: Pony's social worker, Cav, a stone butch; Marie and Stell, both cis female and queer; and Heath, a confident young trans man looking for the father figure he's never had.

Oswald, who came of age in the 1990s and early 2000s, before the vocabulary of trans identity and experience had reached widespread cultural recognition in the United States, has described his ongoing theatrical project as a series of explorations in representing gender nonconformity onstage. Across many plays that investigate and dismantle dramatic genres, this venture has demanded that he interrogate the nature of character, language, landscape, and dramatic structure, and that he lead by example in the realm of theatrical casting. He writes queer and trans characters whose histories and imaginaries splay out across the page in shifting orthographies and alter the barometric pressure for everyone and everything around them. His plots ask how trans experience is recognized and misrecognized, hailed, described, and enacted onstage and onscreen. Trans characters do not need to diarize or confess, in Oswald's works. And if they do enact or verbalize their experience, they do not need to do so in isolation, in realist or linear terms, or using customary vocabularies of transition or paradigms of progress.

Writing these stories—including *Pony* but also multiple other works ranging from *Goat Songs* (2000) to *High Winds* (2017)—without many representational models meant that Oswald was largely alone in building his characters and describing the actors who could play them. As a young writer, he offered readers and directors dramatis personae descriptors like "a boy to be played by a girl."[2] Trans-centered theater initiatives like the Trans Lab (2018) and the Breaking the Binary Theatre Festival (2022) were years away. Lacking more imediate theatrical influences to draw upon, Oswald took inspiration from the early modern dramatic and operatic traditions of the pants or breeches role, English and European theatrical conventions in which female performers wore trousers. These historical models were motivated by conceptions of gender difference that spoke to their own historical contexts. While dominant understandings of seventeenth-century English breeches roles might emphasize their capacity to tantalize male audiences with the silhouette of feminine legs—and male-signifying costumes typically lasted only until the ultimate disclosure of the cis-female character's "true" gender identity—female playwrights like Aphra Behn also used breeches roles to challenge male authority and test the limits of female characters' agency and self-determination.[3] Either way, though, the foundational female identity, coupled with its dramaturgical disclosure late in the play, was precisely not Oswald's goal. His characters wear trousers because that is who they are. If these were not traditional "pants roles," Oswald's graduate school mentor Paula Vogel asked him, then what kinds of roles were they?

As he moved from graduate school at Brown University to New York's downtown theater scene, Oswald began to find inspiration in individual performers—butch, queer, and trans actors of multiple generations—who resonated with the characters populating his theatrical imagination. Peggy Shaw of Split Britches and Dominique Dibbell of the Five Lesbian Brothers provided precedents for butch performance; Oswald has credited Split Britches as a foundational source of inspiration across his body of work. In 2005, he saw the Five Lesbian Brothers' *Oedipus at Palm Springs,* an adaptation of Sophocles's famous tragedy set in a Florida resort with a butch-femme romance at its center. Watching Dominique Dibbell in this production was a revelation: here was a performer, a generation or two removed from Oswald, playing an explicitly butch character whose emotional life was taken seriously as the play's dramatic fuel. Oswald wrote Dibbell a fan letter on pink stationery and, not having Dibbell's mailing address, sent it off to New York Theatre Workshop. Dibbell wrote back.

Meanwhile, at an outdoor performance of the queer troupe Circus Amok, Oswald had encountered trans performer Becca Blackwell, a contemporary, and approached them about working together. He saw actor and director Jess Barbagallo in Big Dance Theater's *The Other Here* at Dance Theater Workshop (2007), and knew he'd encountered an actor who fit his playwriting. A constellation of queer and trans collaborators, spanning multiple generations, began to take shape. Oswald began to see, and to write and stage, a range of genders that looked like, or held dialogue with, his own. (Years later, Barbagallo would direct the production of a revised iteration of *Pony* for the Portland Theater Festival in Portland, Maine, with a primarily local cast that reflected the gender diversity in the play: significant because it demonstrated the increased visibility and availability of butch and trans actors beyond major urban centers like New York.)

In 2006, Oswald read a *New York Times* article titled "The Trouble When Jane Becomes Jack," about the tension between butch lesbians, especially those of an older generation, and the increasingly visible community of young trans men. Hormone care and surgery, still available only to a few, had profoundly altered the scene, and some lesbians felt confused, even betrayed. Barbara Price, once a producer at the Michigan Womyn's Music Festival, and infamous for insisting that attendees be cisgender women only, commented: "Hey, by turning yourselves into men, don't you realize you're going over to the other side? . . . We thought we were all supposed to be in this together."[4] Ten years later, due in part to growing criticism of its trans-exclusionary policies, the festival shuttered its doors. In the intervening time, Oswald had turned his attention to the politics and aesthetics of precisely this generational tension and landscape shift. He devoted himself to writing *Pony*.

Pony features a cast of five characters living five distinctly different genders. They are cis female, trans male, and stone butch. But not one of them is cis male. Encounters place three transmasculine characters of different generations in dialogue with one another: Cav, the oldest, a stone butch; Heath, the youngest, a trans man; and between them, Pony. It might be tempting to read this intergenerational cast list as the blueprint for a narrative of progress, a testament, in the economical form of dramatis personae, to the growing recognition of trans identities and the flourishing of resources for trans people. After all, when Pony inquires about Cav's pronouns, Cav says, "She and her," adding, "It's one thing I never pushed."[5] Heath, by contrast, is a handsome city kid who has had access to hormone care and other forms of acceptance that Cav and Pony did not. He confidently assures Pony that his mom has "gotten used to" his name.[6] Heath scares Cav and annoys Pony: the future bugging the hell out of the past, we might be tempted to think.

But if there is an element of forward motion in this intergenerational drama, a tinge of regret and longing when Cav looks at Heath, Oswald also disrupts any tendency to impose a teleology on Pony's world by arranging the larger play as a landscape of gender, one that tempts us with the possibility of progress but insists on widening horizontally and historically as well. Though there's a love triangle at the play's center, the generational sparks between Cav and Heath—the anxiety and excitement—are as integral to *Pony* as romantic love. Oswald refuses to reject earlier formations of queer female and transmasculine identity as less enlightened, progressive, or significant than current ones, an approach to intergenerational kinship that refutes normative ideas of the nuclear family as the central site of generational inheritance and of linear time as a marker of progress.[7] Rather, the generational model explored in *Pony* evokes Elizabeth Freeman's reevaluation of generational models for queer feminism, expressed in her study *Time Binds*, which was published in 2010—after Oswald had begun writing *Pony* and before its world premiere. Freeman suggests that while feminist philosophy and activism have often been periodized in the form of historically successive "waves," it may be more accurate to understand queer and feminist history as a series of overlapping and multidimensional "forces affected by gravity, which pull backward even as they seem to follow on one another."[8] Linear time and progressive models of political inheritance, she argues, cannot fully account for the complexity of the pull and push among and between generations.

As Oswald wrote, he discovered that *Pony* needed dramatic fuel, a source of action and a structure to propel his protagonist forward. Wandering through a public library in Berkeley, he happened upon a copy of *Woyzeck*, familiar from years of theater study as an early forerunner of the European avant-gardes and as a poster child, in modern dramatic terms, for gendered violence onstage. Büchner's unfinished play, never staged in his lifetime but a powerful influence on modernists a century later, orchestrates a series of exploitative encounters between its title character and the world. A doctor experiments on Woyzeck, a captain issues incessant commands, a handsome drum major tries to seduce away Woyzeck's girlfriend, Marie. Squeezed by the convergence of capitalism, Enlightenment science, and militarism, Woyzeck reenacts the violence that has been inflicted on him by killing Marie. It's a primal scene for modern misogyny and for capitalism's abetting of gendered violence.

In the Berkeley library, Oswald grabbed *Woyzeck* from the shelf, ran off a Xerox, and began a writing exercise called erasure: deleting selected portions of text and making use of what remained. Thus fragments of the already fragmentary play made their way into the foundations of *Pony*, becoming a sedimentary layer that inflects Oswald's play and shapes its characters without serving as an object of adaptation in any simplified way. In Oswald's drama, for instance, there are two Maries. One is not a character but part of the play's exposition, a woman we never meet because she was murdered before the play began. The other Marie—Oswald's Marie, and ours—is a dive-bar waitress obsessively (but unofficially) investigating the crime, not because she wants to "solve" it but because she wants to understand. A love triangle emerges, including Pony and Marie but also Stell, who runs the town newsstand, assists Heath in his search for a trans father figure, and fantasizes about running away with Marie into a world where "All the stupid men will melt / and we can walk north."[9] Then too, *Pony*—like *Woyzeck*—places Marie in a world of gendered violence, but Oswald makes this a deliberately imaginary force, refusing to reproduce the images and actions of male-on-female brutality. Rather than absorbing male anger and male blows, Oswald's Marie fantasizes those things, inventing an abusive boyfriend and playing both his role and hers in a series of solo scenes.

Approaches to gendered violence and the gendered body would evolve as Oswald saw the play in production and as cultural dialogues about trans identity began to raise consciousness in the theater community. *Pony*'s first public reading took place in 2007 at Walkerspace in Tribeca and was produced by Karina Mangu-Ward with Blackwell playing Pony and Barbagallo as Heath. Kate McKinnon of *Saturday Night Live* fame (whom Mangu-Ward had cold-emailed after seeing her on Logo TV's *The Big Gay Sketch Show*) read stage directions. For many involved, the reading was a pivotal moment. Barbagallo and Blackwell met during the rehearsal process and forged a decades-long collaboration. Many collaborators and audience members saw a new vision for what queer and trans theater could look like. Mangu-Ward remembers her excitement at what she, even then, identified as a "new guard" for queer playwriting. Oswald's writing offered "this idea of mixed queer," she recalled. "It wasn't queer women or gay men, it was all gendered, all sexuality. Working with Sylvan was the first time I saw transmasculine people in theater."[10]

That 2007 reading of *Pony* resonated far beyond its immediate audience, bringing together a group of artists and producers who saw the need to support butch and transmasculine performers and to connect them with appropriate theatrical roles. Soon, a venture called the Butch Casting Project took shape, founded by Oswald, Mangu-Ward, and playwright Madeleine George, in collaboration with WP Theater producing artistic director Lisa McNulty (who was, at the time, an artistic line producer with Manhattan Theatre Club). McNulty had long served as an informal agent of sorts, connecting theaters and casting agents with butch performers, and she noted that at the time, casting butch actors of a diverse range of ages was particularly difficult. "An older generation wasn't rewarded for looking that way," she said, "so they left the business, or conformed."[11] The Butch Casting Project was a shoestring endeavor, operated primarily by Mangu-Ward as a Facebook group connecting butch performers to casting opportunities, and casting directors to the performers they sought. Lacking budget, paid staff, and infrastructure, the project eventually languished, but it was still so unique in its field that as late as 2014, Mangu-Ward recalls, casting directors from major Off-Broadway theaters were contacting her for referrals to butch actors.[12]

The Butch Casting Project responded to the needs of plays like *Pony* and Madeleine George's *The Zero Hour*: plays that created profound shifts for many of their casts. For Blackwell, playing Pony provided a rare opportunity to inhabit a complex transmasculine role. "It was really exciting for me to play a role that was written inside of this context of gender performance, and struggle, and having a romantic experience," they remembered. For trans characters, of which there were few to begin with, "none of those things are ever really expressed."[13] Blackwell, Barbagallo, and Mangu-Ward went on to collaborate with Theatre of a Two-Headed Calf's Dyke Division on the three-season serial *Room for Cream*, a theatrical soap opera set in the fictive town of Sappho, Massachusetts, and featuring a range of queer female and transmasculine characters. "I was twenty-four and wanted to make the next guard of queer stuff happen," said Mangu-Ward. "I just wanted to be part of that in whatever way I could."[14]

In 2011, director and producer Bonnie Metzgar staged the world premiere of *Pony* with Chicago's About Face Theatre, an institution dedicated to providing a home for gay and lesbian work. Kelli Simpkins, a Chicago-based actor who had performed in, among other things, Tectonic Theater Project's *The Laramie Project*, played Pony. Casting Heath, even in a queer community, was more difficult. At About Face, Metzgar had founded a festival called XYZ, and the year she produced *Pony*, Oswald's play figured as the festival centerpiece, with a production of *Woyzeck* running in repertory with it and a citywide invitation to artists to propose related projects. There were readings of the play meant to introduce *Pony* to the trans community and invite transmasculine performers to audition for the full production. The actor playing Stell held an open-mic event with her queer choreography trio, and Metzgar gave out *Pony*-themed swag: buttons, temporary tattoos. Even in the queer theater community, though, the play challenged its audience's dramatic and gendered preconceptions. "In some ways our older gay audience needed as much 'Trans 101' as any other audience," Metzgar noted.[15]

Since then, copies of *Pony* have circulated among actors and directors, in rehearsal rooms, and in university classrooms. One day Barbagallo heard from a friend, actor Dave Register, whom he'd met as part of the Broadway cast of *Harry Potter and the Cursed Child*. Register was working with a nonbinary actor in his scene study class and wanted to offer them a substantive role that aligned with their gender. Barbagallo didn't have to think too hard: He sent a copy of *Pony*. Years later, when Register founded a summer theater festival in Portland, Maine, he decided *Pony* would be one of its inaugural productions and invited Barbagallo to direct.

More than simply a second production, this 2022 staging was an event so meaningful for the play and for trans visibility onstage that, during the first rehearsal, Oswald called the production less a revival than a "rebirth." The new production of *Pony* reflected increasing recognition for Oswald's writing and, more broadly, expanded institutional efforts to produce trans stories well beyond New York and to cast trans actors in roles that align with their gender. "For *Pony* to be receiving its second production eleven years after premiering is hugely validating," Oswald told me at the time. Among other things, he pointed out, this meant that there were enough transmasculine actors to fill the roles, and that there was a community ready and waiting for this play, neither of which had been a given even ten years earlier. Also in 2022, a new production at San Francisco's Cutting Ball Theater linked explicitly to its local trans community, partnering with the Transgender District of San Francisco, both a community organization and the first legally recognized transgender district in the world.[16]

The new productions allowed the play new life in the wake of revisions Oswald had made over many years in response to evolving conversations about LGBTQ+ experience. In initial iterations, Pony lived in a remote, run-down town to escape a life where he couldn't be out. After conversations with trans writer Jacob Anderson-Minshall during a 2008 workshop at Portland Center Stage in Oregon, Oswald more clearly understood the implications of presenting trans characters as inextricably trapped in old lives or ashamed to come out. He changed the personal history that propels Pony to the town where he meets Marie, Stell, Cav, and Heath.

More recently, Oswald rethought the play's approach to physical intimacy. In an early draft, Marie unbuttons Pony's shirt and sees his bound chest, which is, for Pony, a deep violation. The 2022 version offers a different possibility. "Because this play is meant to subvert gendered violence, not replicate it, Pony's body shall not be revealed," writes Oswald in stage directions. "Our bodies do not define our gender."[17] Barbagallo reflected on the play's provocative, subtle dialogue about consent and intimacy. "Sylvan always writes with great sensitivity in listening to the vulnerable body," he said. "The crux of the story is: Will I let someone touch me here, will I let someone touch me *here*." Until recently, Barbagallo told me, "there wasn't discourse around that."[18]

Even ten years after its premiere, Barbagallo reflected, the intergenerational queer conversation offered by *Pony* was rare. "Obviously queer theater happens in New York," he said, "but a queer play that has a trans protagonist and that's dealing with the internal politics of being in queer community? This play is fully legible; the dreams of the characters can be followed by anyone. But the shorthand that is happening around this butch-to-transmasculine spectrum—there aren't a lot of plays doing that." It also testifies to real-world artistic encounters and shifts that echo those in the play: Barbagallo recalled that as a young queer actor, playing Heath in that 2007 reading "was part of my edification." Fifteen years later, he reflected, "I'm an elder to that character now."

As Oswald told me, the presence of new productions ten and fifteen years after *Pony*'s initial reading has testified to a critical mass of trans and gender nonconforming actors, directors, and audience members who need this play. The American theater world does too. Oswald's introductory notes to the play text cite an unnamed critic who, after examining the fragmented and unfinished manuscript of *Woyzeck*, wrote, "Strictly speaking, [*this play*] does not exist." *Pony*, and Oswald's playwriting work writ large, reach back and propel forward in personal and historical time, refusing the terms of mere existence and opening out into expansive queer worlds.

NOTES

1. Sylvan Oswald, *Pony*, 91.
2. Sylvan Oswald, *Goat Songs*, unpublished.
3. Diane Torr and Stephen Bottoms, *Sex, Drag, and Male Roles: Investigating Gender as Performance* (University of Michigan Press, 2010), 10–11.
4. Paul Vitello, "The Trouble When Jane Becomes Jack," *New York Times*, August 20, 2006, https://www.nytimes.com/2006/08/20/fashion/20gender.html.
5. Oswald, *Pony*, 16.
6. Oswald, *Pony*, 69.
7. See Jack Halberstam, *Female Masculinity* (Duke University Press, 2018), for essential context on this topic.
8. Elizabeth Freeman, *Time Binds: Queer Temporalities, Queer Histories* (Duke University Press, 2010), 65.
9. Oswald, *Pony*, 61.
10. Karina Mangu-Ward, phone interview with author, August 17, 2023.
11. Lisa McNulty, phone interview with author, September 15, 2023.
12. Mangu-Ward, phone interview with author.
13. Becca Blackwell, phone interview with author, August 1, 2023.
14. Mangu-Ward, phone interview with author.
15. Bonnie Metzgar, phone interview with author, July 14, 2023.
16. See https://www.transgenderdistrictsf.com/about for more information. Accessed August 18, 2023.
17. Oswald, *Pony*, 65.
18. Jess Barbagallo, phone interview with author, July 20, 2022. All subsequent quotations from Barbagallo are from this interview.

ACKNOWLEDGMENTS

Pony's long road has been paved by the trans, queer, and feminist playwrights, ensembles, and performance artists who fought to be heard and the visionary producers who saw the importance of what they had to say.

Writing this play was a yearslong effort kicked off with a fellowship of sorts that I cobbled together in 2005 through donations of housing from Davina Cohen, Stephanie Fleischmann, Sarah Kroll-Rosenbaum, and Steve Moore. And while I can never know the many colleagues who read the play on panels, granting support for my continued work, I am grateful that you took a chance on me. Millay Arts sheltered early writing, and a Thurber House Fellowship through the Ohio State University theater department gave the play its first full public reading in 2006. Additional development support came through a Jerome Fellowship from the Playwrights' Center in Minneapolis and a McCarter Theatre retreat—thank you P. Carl, Carrie Hughes, and Adam Immerwahr. Karina Mangu-Ward produced a pivotal reading at Walkerspace and another at the New York Theatre Workshop directed by Ken Rus Schmoll, who also workshopped the play at Portland Center Stage's JAW West Festival. Gratitude to Mead Hunter for starting with transmasc casting that year, and Rose Riordan for welcoming the play. Morgan Jenness took a risk on me in this early era as my agent at Abrams and offered much inspiration and advice about revision in the run-up to the About Face world premiere, which Bonnie Metzgar directed and produced with great care. I'm still celebrating the Chicago cast's brilliance and Eric Hoff's dramaturgy and fellowship. New Dramatists was my artistic home from 2009 to 2016 and was, until now, one of the few ways a person could access the script for *Pony.* Lily Binns was my partner through much of this time and I am forever grateful for her wisdom and panache.

Rachel Viola has since agented me generously through many aesthetic adventures. Megan Stielstra at Northwestern University Press has offered enthusiasm for this play beyond what I could ever have expected—thank you for seeing its value. My deepest gratitude to Becca Blackwell, Jess Barbagallo, and Zuzanna Szadkowski for their collaboration and for all the ways they've inspired my work beyond *Pony.* I'm thankful to have dear and opinionated friends in Cory Hinkle, Deborah Stein, and Maria Cataldo, who has never steered me wrong. My parents Dianna Marder and Michael Oswald showed me that writing was real work and making art was a way of life. Together with my stepmother Lisa Oswald, their unqualified support afforded me an education that made this life possible. UCLA's School of Theater, Film, and Television has been my base since 2014, and the place where I've found new ways forward on my own terms. Much appreciation to my departmental colleagues for their community.

Miriam Felton-Dansky has been the driving force behind getting this play published and making sure that it was not lost to time. We've been in conversation about theater for over twenty years, but it is the project of our future that may be the best one yet.